Pro Zend Framework Techniques

Build a Full CMS Project

Forrest Lyman

The Zend Press Series

Pro Zend Framework Techniques: Build a Full CMS Project

ISBN-13 (pbk): 978-1-4302-1879-1

ISBN-13 (electronic): 978-1-4302-1880-7

Printed and bound in the United States of America 9 8 7 6 5 4 3 2 1

Trademarked names may appear in this book. Rather than use a trademark symbol with every occurrence of a trademarked name, we use the names only in an editorial fashion and to the benefit of the trademark owner, with no intention of infringement of the trademark.

Lead Editor: Tom Welsh
Technical Reviewer: Adam DeFields
Editorial Board: Clay Andres, Steve Anglin, Mark Beckner, Ewan Buckingham, Tony Campbell, Gary Cornell, Jonathan Gennick, Michelle Lowman, Matthew Moodie, Jeffrey Pepper, Frank Pohlmann, Ben Renow-Clarke, Dominic Shakeshaft, Matt Wade, Tom Welsh
Project Managers: Beth Christmas and Debra Kelly
Copy Editor: Kim Wimpsett
Compositor: v-prompt e-Services
Indexer: BIM Indexing & Proofreading Services
Artist: April Milne

Distributed to the book trade worldwide by Springer-Verlag New York, Inc., 233 Spring Street, 6th Floor, New York, NY 10013. Phone 1-800-SPRINGER, fax 201-348-4505, e-mail orders-ny@springer-sbm.com, or visit http://www.springeronline.com.

For information on translations, please e-mail info@apress.com, or visit http://www.apress.com.

Apress and friends of ED books may be purchased in bulk for academic, corporate, or promotional use. eBook versions and licenses are also available for most titles. For more information, reference our Special Bulk Sales–eBook Licensing web page at http://www.apress.com/info/bulksales.

The source code for this book is available to readers at http://www.apress.com.

I would like to dedicate this book to Johnny,
who first introduced me to the magic that can lie within the covers of a book.

Contents at a Glance

Contents

Preface

Zend Framework has been designed from the ground up to make PHP development as easy – and fun – as possible while promoting best practices and providing an extensible framework for complex applications. Content management systems are a particularly important class of applications – after all, serving content is what the web does best. As the project lead of the Digitalus CMS project, a commercial CMS built on Zend Framework, Forrest Lyman is particularly well-qualified to guide the reader through the involved process of building a full-fledged CMS.

This book reflects the best practices that we have discovered with the help of the Zend Framework community over the last four years. Forrest brings our MVC components to life, while describing data persistence in detail using Zend_Db_Table and MySQL. Essential components for CMSs, such as Zend_Search_Lucene and Zend_Feed, are used to develop ZF modules to implement practical use cases. Finally, he covers advanced topics such as performance optimization and designing your CMS for extension.

Those looking for a guide to using the latest components in Zend Framework will not be disappointed – Zend_Tool, Zend_Navigation, Zend_Application, and more are put to use in the extensive running example CMS application.

This book is the perfect complement to the documentation that can be found on http://framework.zend.com.

Wil Sinclair

About the Author

 Forrest Lyman is a passionate open source developer who splits most of his time between developing dynamic web sites powered by Zend Framework and building systems to make it easier for other people to do the same. He is the creator of the Digitalus CMS open source project, which is a Zend Framework–based content management system. When he is not in front of a computer, he is usually spending time with his girls, Luna and Stella, or searching for tuna offshore.

About the Technical Reviewers

■**Adam DeFields** is a consultant specializing in web application development, project management, technical writing/editing, and instructional design. He lives in Grand Rapids, Michigan, where he runs Emanation Systems, LLC (www.emanationsystemsllc.com), an IT services company he founded in 2002. He has coauthored or reviewed more than a dozen books on various technologies, including Java, PHP, Apache, MySQL, and Zend Framework.

■**Wil Sinclair** is currently working on technologies that facilitate and encourage cloud adoption in the PHP community as the Cloud Strategist at Zend Technologies.

He brings 10 years of experience in the software industry at companies from the smallest startups to the largest multinationals such as Oracle and Amazon. Most recently he served as project lead on the leading PHP framework: Zend Framework.

Acknowledgments

I would like to take a moment to thank everyone who helped make this book possible. When I first proposed the project, I had no idea how much work went into writing, editing, and publishing a book. I don't believe this project would have been possible without all of the support and encouragement I have received.

I would like to start by thanking all of the developers who worked on the Zend Framework project and who guided me through my early days learning new ways to develop software. I was inspired by the support that I got from the team, which gave me the confidence to focus my energy on ZF development.

I would also like to thank the Apress team for sticking it out with me and keeping me on track. They believed in me and the project even when I wasn't sure.

Finally, I would like to thank Wil Sinclair for taking the time to give me a unique perspective into the underlying process that went into the framework's development.

Introduction

This book guides you through the process of developing a content management system with Zend Framework. It utilizes a hands-on, step-by-step approach that introduces you to many of the core components of the framework over the course of the project.

When the project is completed, you will have more than a simple CMS system; you will also have the skills and experience that you need to customize this base to meet the requirements of much more advanced and complicated projects.

Who This Book Is For

This book was written for PHP programmers who have at least some experience working with object-oriented PHP. It would help to have some familiarity with Zend Framework, but you will learn a lot about the framework over the course of the book.

Prerequisites

To follow along with the examples, you will need a computer on which you can install a local testing server. In this book, I use Zend Server Community Edition, which is a free server that comes preconfigured to work seamlessly with the framework.

I strongly recommend a professional IDE such as Zend Studio as well; it is true that many PHP programmers get along fine with a simple text editor, but these object-oriented principles are much easier to manage and develop with the proper software.

CHAPTER 1

■■■

Getting Started

Before you get into building your CMS project, it is important to understand a few things about Zend Framework (ZF). The core of ZF is a loosely coupled application framework that consists of a library of components.

These components are all written in object-oriented PHP, closely following the current best practices. They can be used independently, much like components in many other code libraries. For example, a developer can use the Zend_Service_Amazon component without using the Zend_Db abstraction layer.

What differentiates ZF from many other PHP code bases is the model-view-controller (MVC) implementation. MVC is a pattern where an application is broken into three distinct parts:

- *Business logic*: The controller handles the logic behind the application.

- *Data*: The model handles managing the application data.

- *Presentation*: The view handles rendering the dynamic pages.

Note There are a number of differing opinions regarding the structure of an MVC application. The approach I just described is referred to as the *fat controller* approach.

This pattern is rapidly becoming the standard for web application development, because this clean separation makes complicated sites significantly easier to develop and maintain. This is particularly true in the case of a development team; the developers can focus on their areas of expertise without having to work around unrelated code.

Introducing Zend Framework MVC Implementation

Zend Framework's MVC implementation consists of three main components:

- Zend_Controller

- The model, which often consists of a Zend_Db_Table class but can be any data source

- Zend_View

At its simplest, Zend_Controller processes the request, fetches data from Zend_Db, and then passes this data to Zend_View to render the dynamic XHTML. Bear in mind that ZF is a very flexible framework,

1

and any of these components can be used on their own, but they provide a rich application platform when used together.

The Controller: Zend_Controller_Front

`Zend_Controller_Front` implements the front controller pattern. All requests are ported through this single point of entry, which is responsible for building and returning the response. The front controller's workflow consists of several components, which represent the following sequential process:

1. The request object (`Zend_Controller_Request_Abstract`): This represents the unprocessed request and is responsible for evaluating the user request and providing information about the request to the rest of the process.

2. The router (`Zend_Controller_Router_Interface`): The router inspects the request object and then determines which controller and action should be run to process the request. By default, the router breaks down the URL into the controller, actions, and key/value pairs of parameters. For example, `http://localhost/user/profile/id/234` would be evaluated to the user controller and `profile` action, and the parameter id would equal 234.

3. The dispatcher (`Zend_Controller_Dispatcher_Interface`): The dispatcher takes the information that the router provides, instantiates the proper action controller, and runs the action method. Bear in mind that this process occurs in a loop and can happen several times during the scope of a request. This is commonly used with modular applications that may run several actions prior to returning the response. I often use this approach to enable developers to embed the response from a module in a CMS page.

4. The response (`Zend_Controller_Response_Abstract`): The response object is responsible for collecting and returning the responses from the controller actions.

The Model: Zend_Db

A web application can serve data from many sources, but the most common source is a database. `Zend_Db` provides a SQL database interface for ZF. A number of adapters for different database systems are available that provide an abstraction layer to these databases. This abstraction layer enables you to use a common set of tools for a range of different database systems.

`Zend_Db_Table`, which is the class that you will use to create your models, provides an object-oriented interface to these database tables. It implements the Table Data Gateway pattern. This pattern manages all the SQL for common database functions. This is a more generic approach to database abstraction, as opposed to other ORM systems that map data objects and their relationships to a relational database.

It also includes an implementation of the Row Data Gateway pattern, which creates data objects that provide access to all the underlying information in a database row.

The View: Zend_View

Zend_View is a lightweight class that provides the view for the ZF MVC implementation. The front controller creates an instance of Zend_View, which maps to the action methods in the controller classes. The action method sets view variables with data that it loads from the model, and then Zend_View takes this data and generates the XHTML response. It includes a number of tools to make this process as flexible as possible, including helpers and filters. Bear in mind that although Zend_View uses PHP as its default template system, you can use it with a variety of different systems such as Smarty.

Setting Up Your Development Environment

The first thing you will need to set up for the framework is a development server to build and test your projects on. There are a wide range of options for both Linux and Windows operating systems. One of these solutions, which includes Zend Framework and command-line tools, is Zend Server. There are two versions of this package: the community version and a commercial version that includes support, updates, and additional features. For your local development environment, the community version should suffice.

Installing Zend Server CE

Zend Server includes installers for both Linux and Windows. In this section, I will describe the installation process for the Windows version.

First you need to get download the server installer. You can get the current download on the Zend Server website (http://www.zend.com/en/products/server/).

Once you have downloaded the installer, start it, and you should see a screen that looks like Figure 1-1.

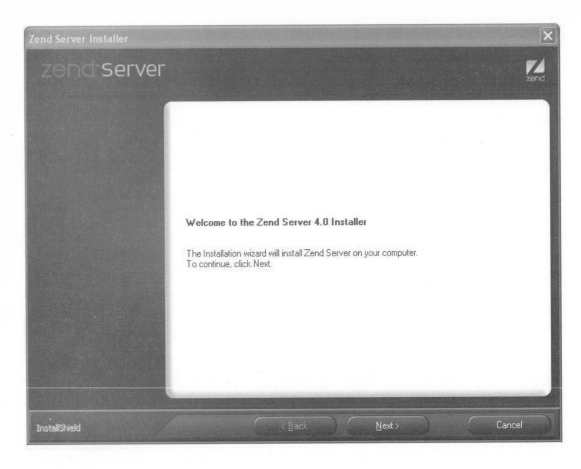

Figure 1-1. The Zend Server Windows installer

Click Next, and then read and agree to the license. Next you will be prompted to choose an installation type. Select Custom, and click Next.

You can select any components that you want, but make sure that the following items are selected:

PHP

- Common Extensions
- Additional Extensions

Zend Framework

- Base
- Extras

MySQL server

Once you have set up your components, click Next. Now select the option install the Apache server, and click Next. The next step is to select the port for Apache to use. In most situations, you can just use the default, port 80. Click Next and then Install to install the server. This may take some time because there are a number of components that need to be downloaded before your installation can be completed. Once the installation is completed, the installer will give you the option of starting to work with Zend Server. Select this option, and click Finish. Your browser should open, and you will be directed to the server administration page. The first time you load the server administration page, Zend Server will prompt you for a password. Once you enter the password, you will be granted access to the main server administration console.

Doing Rapid Application Development with the Zend Command-Line Tool

The Zend command-line tool gives developers access to the Zend Tool Framework through the command-line interface. Zend Tool Project provides a number of tools for creating new projects and adding components to existing projects.

Zend Tool Project is configured as part of the Zend Server installation, but it is not difficult to manually configure it if you are not using Zend Server. Consult the documentation for Zend Framework for more information on this subject.

Next open a terminal window. Next check the current version of the framework using the `zf show version` command. If everything is properly set up, you should see `Zend Framework Version: 1.8.x`, as in Figure 1-2.

Figure 1-2. Running the `zf show version` command

The Zend Tool Framework uses one of two files:

- zf.bat for Windows users

- zf.sh for Unix users

The usage of these two commands is identical. In the examples in this book, I will use the Windows version, because I develop on Windows. For Unix-based developers, simply replace zf.bat with zf.sh.

Creating Your Project

Now that you have your development environment installed and tested, you are ready to start building the project.

Building a Project with the Zend Tool Framework

To build your project, open your terminal window. Then navigate to your server's document root. The document root is the folder that contains all the publicly accessible scripts on your server; in a default Zend Server installation, this will be ~/Apache2/htdocs. You create a new project using the create project command. Follow this command with the name of your project, which in this case will be zf_cms. Run this command, and the Zend Tool Framework will build the base project, as in Figure 1-3.

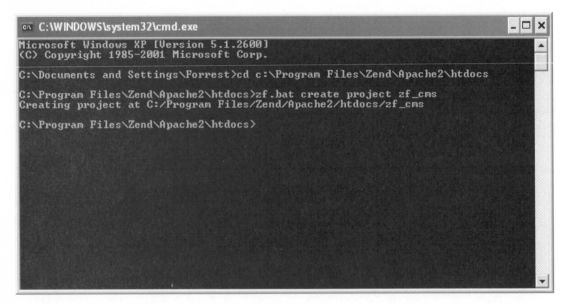

Figure 1-3. Creating a project with the Zend Tool Framework

Testing Your New Project

Now if you point your browser to http://localhost/zf_cms/public, you will see the welcome page.

To make the rest of your development process easier, set the server's document root to this folder. To set the document root, locate your httpd.conf file, which is in the Apache2/conf folder. Open this file in a text editor, and then locate the DocumentRoot directive. Update it with the absolute path to the public folder of your project, as in Listing 1-1.

■ **Note** I often set up vhosts using the httpd-vhosts.conf file. This enables you to create multiple *virtual hosts* on your server, which behave more or less like independent servers. This enables me to manage multiple development sites on a single server instance.

Listing 1-1. Updating the Document Root in Apache2/conf/httpd.conf

```
DocumentRoot "{absolute path to apache}/Apache2/htdocs/zf_cms/public"
```

You also need to enable rewriting in the zf_cms folder. Add the directive shown in Listing 1-2 to the end of the httpd.conf file, replacing {absolute path to apache} with the root-relative path to your server instance.

Listing 1-2. Configuring the zf_cms Project in Apache2/conf/httpd.conf

```
<Directory "{absolute path to apache}\Apache2\htdocs\zf_cms">
    Options Indexes FollowSymLinks
    AllowOverride All
    Order allow,deny
    Allow from all
</Directory>
```

Once you have updated this directive, restart your server, and point your browser to http://localhost again. Now you should see your project rather than the Zend Server welcome screen (Figure 1-4).

Figure 1-4. *Zend Framework project welcome screen*

Exploring the Anatomy of Your Project

If you open the folder that the Zend Tool Framework created for your project, you will see that the project is organized into three subfolders:

- public: All the files that must be publicly accessible will reside in this folder, which will be your document root.

- library: This folder will contain the framework's library as well as a custom library that you will create for this project.

- application: This folder is the heart of your project. It is where your models, views, and controllers will be.

You should note that ZF is not nearly as strict as many other application frameworks. This structure represents the standard layout of a ZF application, so many aspects of the framework will work without overriding the default behavior. At the same time, you can customize almost every aspect of the framework to work the way you want it to work. I prefer the "convention over configuration" approach, so I tend to stick with the defaults whenever possible.

The public Folder

The public folder is your document root. Zend Framework follows current best security practices by not exposing any of the core executable files to the public. The only files that are kept in the public web root are files that the browser must be able to access.

Redirecting the Request with .htaccess

When a new request comes to your project, the server loads the .htaccess file (Listing 1-3). The .htaccess file does two things. First it sets the APPLICATION_ENV environmental variable. This enables you to manage multiple environments in the application, which can be configured independently. Once this is set, it redirects every request (that does not map to an existing file) to the index.php file.

Listing 1-3. The .htaccess file in /public/.htaccess

```
SetEnv APPLICATION_ENV development
RewriteEngine On
RewriteCond %{REQUEST_FILENAME} -s [OR]
RewriteCond %{REQUEST_FILENAME} -l [OR]
RewriteCond %{REQUEST_FILENAME} -d
RewriteRule ^.*$ - [NC,L]
RewriteRule ^.*$ index.php [NC,L]
```

The Index File

When the index.php file (Listing 1-4) receives the request, it builds the application and runs it.

First, it defines the default APPLICATION_PATH and APPLICATION_ENV environment variables. This is important because .htaccess might not be loaded, depending on the request type (a cron job, for example).

Next it ensures that the library is included in the project. At this point, the library is empty, because the Zend Framework library is included by your php.ini file.

Then it creates a new instance of Zend_Application, passing it the APPLICATION_ENV environment variable and the path to the application configuration file. This file is where you define how the application will be built.

Finally, it calls the Zend_Application instance's bootstrap() method and runs the application.

Listing 1-4. The index.php File in public/index.php

```php
<?php
// Define path to application directory
defined('APPLICATION_PATH')
    || define('APPLICATION_PATH', realpath(dirname(__FILE__) . '/../application'));
// Define application environment
defined('APPLICATION_ENV')
    || define('APPLICATION_ENV', (getenv('APPLICATION_ENV') ?
    getenv('APPLICATION_ENV') : 'production'));
// Ensure library/ is on include_path
```

```
set_include_path(implode(PATH_SEPARATOR, array(
    realpath(APPLICATION_PATH . '/../library'),
    get_include_path(),
)));
/** Zend_Application */
require_once 'Zend/Application.php';
// Create application, bootstrap, and run
$application = new Zend_Application(
    APPLICATION_ENV,
    APPLICATION_PATH . '/configs/application.ini'
);
$application->bootstrap()
            ->run();
```

Additional Public Folders

At this point you should also add three other subfolders in the public folder: images, css, and javascript. Depending on your application, you may need to add other folders to this, such as one for document downloads.

The library Folder

I prefer to install the library in each project. This is because you may run several ZF projects on a single server, and different projects may be built on different versions of the framework.

Download the most recent version of the framework at http://framework.zend.com. Extract the archive contents, and then copy the Zend folder from the download's library folder into your library folder. The framework is simply a library of classes, so you don't need to perform any other installation procedures.

You will be creating several library classes for the CMS project, and it is a best practice to create your own library folder to do this so your code does not get mixed up with the ZF core. Create a new folder in the library called CMS. Your library folder should look like Listing 1-5.

Listing 1-5. The library Folder

```
/ library
    / Zend
    / CMS
```

The application Folder

The application folder is where all of your models, views, and controllers are located. This keeps all of your business logic outside the publicly accessible document root.

Zend_Application

As web applications become more advanced, they also become more complicated to manage. In previous versions of the framework, this was handled by a number of files and plug-ins, which were responsible for different areas of the process. Zend_Application provides an object-oriented method for configuring, bootstrapping, and running ZF applications.

The Bootstrap Class

The Bootstrap class (Listing 1-6), by default, initializes the front controller and uses the default application/controllers path as the path to the controllers. As you build your CMS, you will add many more *resources* to the Bootstrap class, such as the database connection, but for now this is a very simple class that leverages the base Zend_Application_Bootstrap_Bootstrap functionality.

Listing 1-6. The Bootstrap Class in application/Bootstrap.php

```php
<?php
class Bootstrap extends Zend_Application_Bootstrap_Bootstrap {}
```

Application Configuration

The Zend Tool Framework created the default site configuration file (Listing 1-7) in application/configs/application.ini.

When you open this file, you will notice that four config sections are defined. Each of these sections relates to an application environment. This enables you to configure your different environments independently. For example, you probably want to display any errors that occur on the development environment, but not on the production site. You will also notice that staging, testing, and development extend production using the following coding convention: [testing : production]. This enables you to set your core application settings in the base section and then override any settings that are different in the specific sections.

By default, this config file sets the following:

- PHP error settings

- Additional application include paths

- The path to the bootstrap class

- The bootstrap class name

- The path to the default controller directory

As you build this CMS project, you will add many more settings to this file.

Listing 1-7. The Default Application Config File in application/configs/application.ini

```
[production]
phpSettings.display_startup_errors = 0
phpSettings.display_errors = 0
includePaths.library = APPLICATION_PATH "/../library"
bootstrap.path = APPLICATION_PATH "/Bootstrap.php"
bootstrap.class = "Bootstrap"
resources.frontController.controllerDirectory = APPLICATION_PATH "/controllers"
```

```
[staging : production]

[testing : production]
phpSettings.display_startup_errors = 1
phpSettings.display_errors = 1

[development : production]
phpSettings.display_startup_errors = 1
phpSettings.display_errors = 1
```

Action Controllers

The action controllers manage your application. When you run the application, it processes the request, loads the appropriate controller class, and then runs the action that was requested. The action, in turn, loads and processes any required data from the models and then renders the proper view script.

The Zend Tool Framework creates the IndexController class (Listing 1-8), which is the default controller. At this point, IndexController and indexAction() are simply handing control over to Zend Framework. Later in the book, when you are building the actual CMS, you will add the application logic to these action methods.

Listing 1-8. The IndexController Class in application/controllers/IndexController.php

```php
<?php
class IndexController extends Zend_Controller_Action
{
    public function init()
    {
        /* Initialize action controller here */
    }
    public function indexAction()
    {
        // action body
    }
}
```

Views

Once indexAction() hands the control over, the framework will map the request to the view scripts and render this as the response. By default the framework will look for a view script named index.phtml (Listing 1-9) in the /views/scripts/index folder that resides in the same folder as your /controllers folder.

Note the .phtml file extension; using this file extension is the current best practice in Zend Framework development. It differentiates the view scripts from standard PHP files.

Listing 1-9. The index.phtml *View Script in* application/views/scripts/index/index.phtml

```
<style>
    a:link,
    a:visited
    {
        color: #0398CA;
    }
    span#zf-name
    {
        color: #91BE3F;
    }
    div#welcome
    {
        color: #FFFFFF;
        background-image: url(http://framework.zend.com/images/bkg_header.jpg);
        width:  600px;
        height: 400px;
        border: 2px solid #444444;
        overflow: hidden;
    }
    div#more-information
    {
        background-image: url(http://framework.zend.com/images/bkg_body-bottom.gif);
        height: 100%;
    }
</style>
<center>
    <div id="welcome">
        <center>
        <br />
        <h1>Welcome to the <span id="zf-name">Zend Framework!</span><h1 />
        <h3>This is your project's main page<h3 /><br /><br />
        <div id="more-information">
            <br />
            <img src="http://framework.zend.com/images/PoweredBy_ZF_4LightBG.png" />
            <br /><br />
            Helpful Links: <br />
            <A href="http://framework.zend.com/">Zend Framework Website</a> |
            <A href="http://framework.zend.com/manual/en/">Zend Framework Manual</a>
        </div>
    </div>
</center>
```

Error Handling

It is probably safe to assume that everything worked fine in this simplistic example, but errors are a fact of life in programming. Zend Framework includes an error plug-in that handles these issues.

The error plug-in captures any exceptions that are thrown by your application. This includes the exceptions that occur when a controller or action is not found as well as any exceptions that occur in your action controllers. These exceptions relate to 404 and 500 errors.

Once the error plug-in encounters an exception, it redirects the request to ErrorController's errorAction() in the default module. At that point, it hands the control over to you, which enables you to determine how much information to give the user about the issue and how to present it.

The Zend Tool Framework creates the ErrorController class (Listing 1-10) and its associated view (Listing 1-11) for you.

The error controller's errorAction() fetches the error handler and evaluates which type of error occurred. Then it sets the response code and sets the error message. It also passes the exception and the request object to the view, so the view has all the information required to display a complete error report.

Listing 1-10. The ErrorController in application/controllers/ErrorController.php

```php
<?php
class ErrorController extends Zend_Controller_Action
{
    public function errorAction()
    {
        $errors = $this->_getParam('error_handler');
        switch ($errors->type) {
            case Zend_Controller_Plugin_ErrorHandler::EXCEPTION_NO_CONTROLLER:
            case Zend_Controller_Plugin_ErrorHandler::EXCEPTION_NO_ACTION:

                // 404 error -- controller or action not found
                $this->getResponse()->setHttpResponseCode(404);
                $this->view->message = 'Page not found';
                break;
            default:
                // application error
                $this->getResponse()->setHttpResponseCode(500);
                $this->view->message = 'Application error';
                break;
        }
        $this->view->exception = $errors->exception;
        $this->view->request    = $errors->request;
    }
}
```

The error view script renders the error message that was set in the error controller. If the current environment is development, it also renders the complete exception, the stack trace, and any request parameters that were set. This makes it easier for you to track down the issue.

Listing 1-11. The Error View Script in application/views/scripts/error/error.phtml

```
<!DOCTYPE html PUBLIC "-//W3C//DTD XHTML 1.0 Strict//EN";
    "http://www.w3.org/TR/xhtml1/DTD/xhtml1-strict.dtd>
<html xmlns="http://www.w3.org/1999/xhtml">
<head>
  <meta http-equiv="Content-Type" content="text/html; charset=utf-8" />
  <title>Zend Framework Default Application</title>
</head>
<body>
  <h1>An error occurred</h1>
  <h2><?= $this->message ?></h2>

  <? if ('development' == APPLICATION_ENV): ?>

  <h3>Exception information:</h3>
  <p>
      <b>Message:</b> <?= $this->exception->getMessage() ?>
  </p>

  <h3>Stack trace:</h3>
  <pre><?= $this->exception->getTraceAsString() ?>
  </pre>

  <h3>Request Parameters:</h3>
  <pre><? var_dump($this->request->getParams()) ?>
  </pre>
  <? endif ?>
</body>
</html>
```

Now when you point your browser to a page that does not exist, such as
http://localhost/missing/page, you will be directed to this view, which should display your error like
Figure 1-5.

Figure 1-5. The error page

Summary

In this chapter, you set up your development server and created the base for your CMS project, learning about many of the most important Zend Framework components and concepts in the process. Over the course of the rest of this book, you will add more complex designs, database access, interactivity, and security to these simplistic roots. Many of these items may seem complicated at the outset, but always bear in mind that these simple concepts are the basis for every Zend Framework MVC application, no matter how complex.

CHAPTER 2

Designing Your Site

In this chapter, you'll create the template for your CMS using Zend_View and Zend_Layout, which make up the presentation layer for the Zend Framework.

Rendering the Presentation Layer with Zend_View

The core purpose of the Zend_View class is to separate this presentation code from the application logic and data. Separating the HTML from your core application code makes all your code easier to read and follow.

View Scripts

The view scripts are basically PHP files that are rendered within the scope of Zend_View. As such, you can use any of the standard PHP that you need to create your dynamic templates. This is one of the things that I like best about the framework; it gives you a rich set of tools to help with common challenges but allows you to use the tools you are already comfortable with as well.

Rendering your view scripts is a two-stage process. First, the action controller creates a new instance of Zend_View (which is done with its view renderer action helper), which you load with data in your action method. Second, once the action method has been processed, the view renderer helper tells Zend_View to render the appropriate view script. Zend_View takes control from this point and renders the actual view scripts, returning the response to the controller's response segment.

View Helpers

In many situations, you need to do the same repetitive coding tasks many times over the course of a project. The Zend Framework developers anticipated this and created a system of helpers that allow you to create reusable widgets and functions that you can use throughout your view scripts.

Behind the scenes, the helpers are simply classes. When you call a helper from within your script, Zend_View creates a new instance of the class and then runs the method that is relates to the helper class name, named using the *camelCase* convention. For example, MyHelper will run the myHelper() method. Zend_View then returns the response from this method.

The framework ships with a good number of helpers, which include tools to render form controls, run different actions and embed the results, add JavaScript functionality, and much more.

Rendering the Presentation Layer with Zend_Layout

Zend_Layout utilizes the "two-step" view pattern, which enables you to create templates that wrap your individual view scripts. This standardizes your site's look and feel. It also makes it much easier to manage design components that are used sitewide.

Using Zend_Layout on Its Own

Zend_Layout allows you to name sections of your site templates and then load these from within your controller and view scripts. For example, you may have a common header for an entire controller, while each action will generally render the page body.

Zend_Layout MVC

Zend_Layout comes into its own when you use its MVC component. This component includes a front controller plug-in and action helper, which tightly integrate the layout with the front controller.

You start the Zend_Layout MVC by calling its static startMvc() method. You can pass this method an array of configuration options. At a minimum, I generally set the following:

- layout: This is the layout script to render. Note that Zend_Layout will add the .phtml extension to your name, so pass this option layout instead of layout.phtml.

- layoutPath: This is the path to the layout scripts.

Once you have started the Zend_Layout MVC, you can access the layout throughout your controller and view scripts:

- In the controllers, you access the instance using the controller plug-in: $this->_helper->layout.

- In the view, you use the view helper: $this->layout().

Note The controller plug-in does more than just provide access to the layout; it also sets a layout variable for each named segment of the response.

Three-Step Views

Zend_Layout adds continuity to your site layout and can manage the look and feel as well. This works but leaves something to be desired.

It is quite common to have a standard layout for a site and unique features for each site section. Examples I have run into range from a different header graphic for a news section to a completely distinctive look for an e-commerce checkout page.

The solution to this is utilizing skins. Skins manage the look and feel of your site with CSS and graphics files. You simply switch the skin when you want to modify the design but not the layout. See Figure 2-1 to visualize how the page is built using this three-step approach.

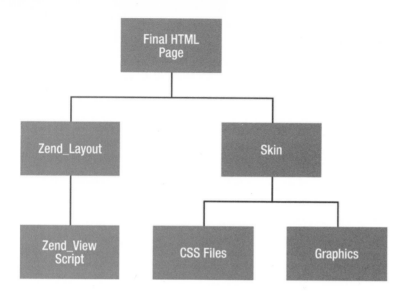

Figure 2-1. *Three-step views with* Zend_View, Zend_Layout, *and skins*

Designing the Interface

Design can be a very frustrating and intimidating task for programmers. In my opinion, a great deal of this boils down to one of the most striking differences between programming and design:

- The foundation of programming is binary logic; there is a right and wrong way to implement a given algorithm.

- The foundation of design is how your brain interprets what it sees; since everyone interprets things differently, it is impossible to say whether something is right or wrong.

This is obviously an oversimplification that does not account for the fact that there are many situations in programming where something technically works but could be improved upon. On the other side of the coin, quite a few design principles are cut and dried.

Using the three-step view pattern, you separate all the application code from the final presentation layer. This allows you to focus on one thing at a time, which makes both the programming and the design easier. It also enables you to change the look and feel of the site without altering the view scripts themselves. I will use this approach in the CMS's templating system in the examples, focusing on the layout structure first and then talking about the look and feel later in the process.

Organizing the Interface Components

Before you can put pen to paper and start designing the interface, it is important to determine the current requirements of the interface. Initially, you need the following areas:

- The site header

- The main site menu

- The main content area

- The site submenu

- The site administrator's menu

- The user login form

- The site footer

The next step is determining how these blocks will fit into the interface. The focus in this chapter is on the techniques that are used in building a template, so I will use a straightforward two-column layout for the example, as in Figure 2-2.

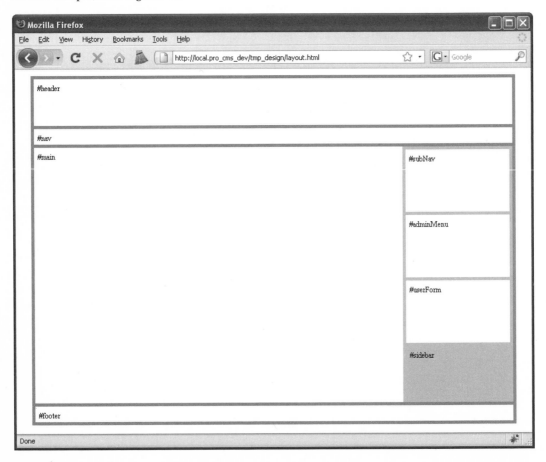

Figure 2-2. A standard two-column layout

Now it is only a matter of choosing where to put the interface components (see Table 2-1).

Table 2-1. The Main Components of the Site Template

Area	Components
Header	The site header The main site menu
Main Content	The main content area
Sidebar	The site submenu The site administrator's menu The user login form
Footer	The site footer

Once this is laid out, you are ready to mock it up.

Mocking It Up

The first step in building a template is to create a mock design. This can take many forms. Many successful web programmers work from sketches, but I prefer the more conventional approach of creating the design using a graphic design program. The key reason for this is that you are able use this working design as both a reference and the base for the graphical elements for your site.

First create a wireframe, which is essentially a line drawing with dimensions. It is important to take care when creating this wireframe so you can measure elements accurately. For reference, I like to add labels to the blocks in the wireframe with their permanent ID and dimensions. See Figure 2-3 for the wireframe of the CMS interface.

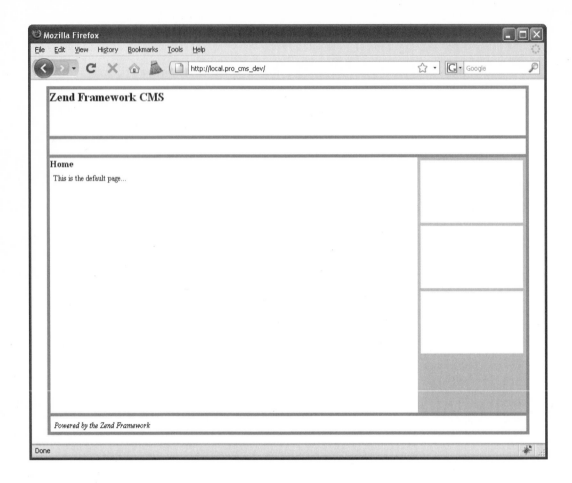

Figure 2-3. *The CMS interface wireframe*

Creating the Base HTML Page

I generally create a temporary folder in the public folder to build and test the base HTML page. Create a new folder in your public folder named temp_design. Add two subfolders to this, images and css, just like the main public folder. Then add a CSS file named style.css to the css folder, and add an HTML file named layout.html to the root of the temp_design folder (see Listing 2-1).

Listing 2-1. *The Temporary Static Design Folder*

```
/ public
    / temp_design
        / images
        / css
```

```
      / style.css
  / layout.html
```

Next open the layout.html file in your editor, and add the base page HTML (Listing 2-2). This includes the header, the main content area, and the sidebar, which contains an area for the submenu, the administrator menu, and the administrator login form. Note that I don't worry about any head elements except the link to the style sheet at this time; I will use the Zend_View placeholders for these.

Note A number of PHP IDEs are available that can accelerate your PHP development and make it easier to develop more stable code. I personally use Zend Studio because it integrates with Zend Server and Zend Framework. PDT is a free Eclipse-based option that I have used as well.

Listing 2-2. The HTML for the Design in public/tmp_design/layout.html

```html
<html>
<head>
    <meta http-equiv="Content-Type" content="text/html; charset=UTF-8" />
    <link href="css/style.css" media="all" rel="stylesheet" type="text/css" />
</head>
<body>
    <div id="pageWrapper">
        <div id="header">
        <p>#header</p>
        </div>
        <div id="nav">
            <p>#nav</p>
        </div>
        <div id="sidebar">
            <div id="subNav">
                <p>#subNav</p>
            </div>
            <div id="adminMenu">
                <p>#adminMenu</p>
            </div>
            <div id="userForm">
                <p>#userForm</p>
            </div>
            <p>#sidebar</p>
        </div>
        <div id="main">
            <p>#main</p>
        </div>
        <div id="footer">
            <p>#footer</p>
        </div>
    </div>
```

```
</body>
</html>
```

Next open the style sheet. The finer points of CSS-based layout are beyond the scope of this book, so I will just show you how I do it (see Listing 2-3).[1] Here are a few keys for me:

- I like to use relative measurements in layouts so people can resize the page as they want. I use the 10 pixel trick (if the font size is 10 pixels, then 1 em = 10 pixels) to make calculating this easier.

- I temporarily set some fixed dimensions early that will become fluid later. This is to help me visualize the page.

- I use the same colors for the elements as I did in the wireframe.

- I like to display the element's ID for reference sake.

Listing 2-3. The Design's CSS in public/tmp_design/layout.css

```
@CHARSET "ISO-8859-1";

body {
    font-size: 10px;
}

* {
    margin: 0;
    padding: 0;
}

p {
    padding: .5em;
    font-size: 1.2em;
}

#pageWrapper {
    background: #999;
    width: 79em;
    margin: 1em auto;
    padding: .5em;
}

#header {
    background: #fff;
    height: 7.5em;
    margin: 0 0 .5em 0;
}
```

---

[1] For detailed advice on CSS layout, see Craig Grannell's *The Essential Guide to CSS and HTML Web Design* (friends of ED, 2007).

```
#nav {
    background: #fff;
    height: 2.5em;
    margin: 0 0 .5em 0;
}

#sidebar {
    background: #ccc;
    float: right;
    width: 17em;
    height: 40em;
    margin: 0 0 .5em .5em;
    padding: .5em;
}

#main {
    background: #fff;
    height: 41em;
    margin: 0 0 .5em 0;
}

#subNav,#adminMenu,#userForm {
    background: #fff;
    width: 17em;
    height: 10em;
    margin: 0 0 .5em 0;
}

#footer {
    clear: both;
    background: #fff;
    height: 2.5em;
    margin: 0;
}
```

Testing Your Design

Now your page is ready to be previewed in the browser. Navigate to
http://localhost/tmp_design/layout.html. The page should look like the wireframe, as shown in Figure
2-4.

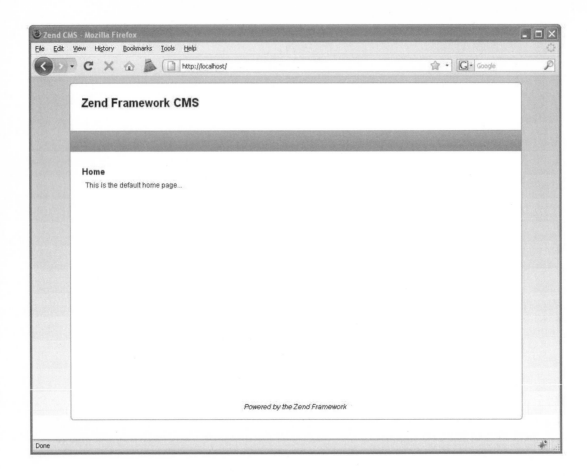

Figure 2-4. The completed HTML layout

Creating the Layout

Now that the HTML design is done, you can roll up your sleeves and get back to the CMS. You need to turn the static HTML design into a Zend_Layout. Since you already have a layout that works, this is going to take only a minute of cutting and pasting.

Creating the Layout

The first step is to move the design files into their permanent locations in the CMS. Once the files are moved, you will rename them. You will name the CSS file after the layout so it is easy to make the association.

1. Create a new folder in the application folder named layouts.

2. Add a subfolder to the layouts folder named scripts.

3. Copy the layout.html file to the application/layouts/scripts folder, and then rename it to layout.phtml.

4. Move the style.css file from public/tmp_design to public/css, and then rename it to layout.css.

5. Delete the public/tmp_design folder.

Adding the Dynamic Head with Zend_View's Placeholders

Now that the files are in place, open the layout.phtml file in your editor. The first thing you need to do is set up the page head. This will be done using the Zend_View placeholder helper. This helper enables you to pass content between view scripts. There are several concrete implementations of the placeholder helpers that ship with the framework:

- Doctype: This renders the proper doctype declaration.

- HeadLink: This adds links to the head, such as links to style sheets.

- HeadMeta: This is used to add metadata about your document.

- HeadScript: This helper is used to add JavaScript to the document. It can be used for both inline and linked files.

- HeadStyle: This helper is used to add inline CSS styles. Use the HeadLink helper to link to a style sheet.

- HeadTitle: This is used to add the document title.

You will use several of these helpers to create the <head> section of the layout. First set the doctype before the HTML, as shown in Listing 2-4.

Listing 2-4. Setting the Doctype in application/layouts/layout.phtml

```php
<?php
echo '<?xml version="1.0" encoding="UTF-8" ?>';
echo $this->doctype();
?>
```

Then you need to replace the static <head> section in the template with a dynamic block that will render the site title, scripts, and style sheets, as shown in Listing 2-5.

Listing 2-5. Setting Up the Page Head in application/layouts/layout.phtml

```php
<head>
<meta http-equiv="Content-Type" content="text/html; charset=UTF-8" />
    <?php
    echo $this->headTitle();
    echo $this->headScript();
```

```
    // add a link to the site style sheet
    $this->headLink()->appendStylesheet('/css/layout.css');
    echo $this->headLink();
    ?>
</head>
```

Adding the Dynamic Content to Your Layout

Now you are ready to add the dynamic content to your layout file. You do this by rendering layout variables in each of the sections that you will need to be able to manipulate; you can use the view layout() helper to do this. This helper fetches the current layout instance and then returns it. This allows you to use the fluent interface, calling the variable directly from the helper call, like $this->layout()->variable.

Replace the entire layout.phtml file's <body> section with the code in Listing 2-6.

Listing 2-6. Rendering Content Using Custom Placeholders in application/layouts/layout.phtml

```
<body>
    <div id="pageWrapper">
        <div id="header">
            <h1>Zend Framework CMS</h1>
        </div>
        <div id="nav">
            <?php echo $this->layout()->nav;?> 
        </div>
        <div id="sidebar">
        <div id="subNav">
            <?php echo $this->layout()->subNav;?> 
        </div>
        <div id="adminMenu">
            <?php echo $this->layout()->adminMenu;?> 
        </div>
        <div id="userForm">
            <?php echo $this->layout()->userForm;?> 
        </div>
        </div>
        <div id="main">
            <?php echo $this->layout()->content?> 
        </div>
        <div id="footer">
            <p><em>Powered by the Zend Framework</em></p>
        </div>
    </div>
</body>
```

Rendering the Controller Response with Zend_Layout

When you use the MVC components of Zend_Layout, each of the named segments of the controller response is set as a layout variable. The default segment is the *content* segment, where the main output from the controller is saved. These segments make it easy to create modular applications; the layout controller helper fetches each of the named segments of the response and assigns them to layout variables. For example, if you forwarded to the nav controller's render action, the layout helper would set the nav variable to the response from the nav controller.

Configuring Your Application to Use the Layout

Now that you have created this layout, you need to update your application so it utilizes your layout script.

First you need to update `application/configs/application.ini`, adding the layout resource to the production section, as shown in Listing 2-7.

Listing 2-7. Adding the Layout Resource to application/configs/application.ini

```
resources.layout.layoutPath = APPLICATION_PATH "/layouts/scripts"
```

Now if you navigate to `http://localhost`, you will see that the entire Zend Framework welcome page is rendering within your layout. Open `application/views/scripts/index/index.phtml`, and replace the welcome page with a simple headline and teaser, as shown in Listing 2-8.

Listing 2-8. The Home Page View in application/views/scripts/index/index.phtml

```
<h2>Home</h2>
<p>This is the default home page...</p>
```

Testing Your New Layout

Now that the layout is complete, you are ready to test it within the scope of your Zend Framework project. Once this is set, you are ready to test the layout in the browser. Navigate to `http://localhost`. The page should look like the static HTML design, with the default page message, as in Figure 2-5.

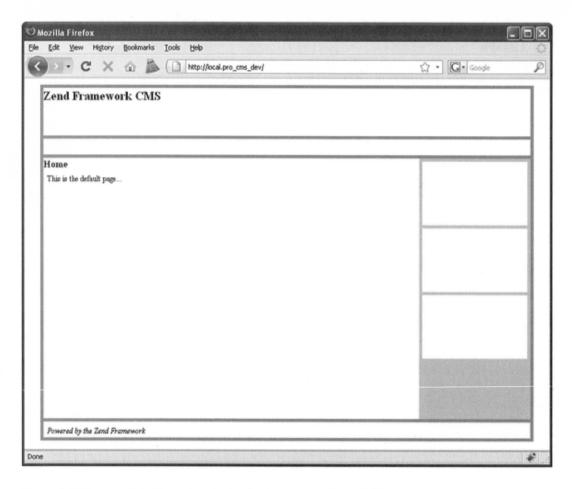

Figure 2-5. The completed layout rendering the home page of the CMS

Implementing the Skin

Now that the layout is implemented, the site is starting to take shape, but the design clearly leaves something to be desired. Zend_View and Zend_Layout do a good job of handling rendering dynamic XHTML; in this section, you'll add onto this functionality by creating a helper that will handle adding skins to your XHTML pages.

What Goes in a Skin?

A skin consists of the CSS style sheets and graphics that add the look and feel to the layout. There are no hard and fast rules regarding what can and cannot be defined in the skin; you will notice, for example, that in this skin you will be overriding some of the base dimensions in the layout.

Creating the Blues Skin

The first thing you need to do to set up your skin is to create a new folder in the /public folder named skins. Next create a folder in that folder named blues for your blues skin.

The skins consist of CSS files and graphics. Create two new folders in the skins/blues folder: one named images and one named css.

Next you need to add the required files to the skin. To start, add two style sheets: one named layout.css and one named text.css. In this CMS, the skins will also contain a skin.xml file, which will tell the loadSkin() helper information about the skin, such as which style sheets to load.

When you are done, your skin folder should contain the folders and files shown in Listing 2-9.

Listing 2-9. The Blues Skin

```
/ public
    / skins
        / blues
            / css
                / layout.css
                / text.css
            / images
            / skin.xml
```

The skin.xml File

At this point, the skin.xml file will just contain a list of style sheets. Note that the loadSkin() helper will load these in order, so you can manipulate the CSS *cascade*. Open the skin.xml file in your editor and your skin's style sheets, as in Listing 2-10.

Note The skin.xml file is not a standard XML schema; it is solely used for this project.

Listing 2-10. Adding the Skin Styles in public/skins/blues/skin.xml

```
<?xml version="1.0" encoding="UTF-8"?>
<skin>
    <stylesheets>
        <stylesheet>layout.css</stylesheet>
        <stylesheet>text.css</stylesheet>
    </stylesheets>
</skin>
```

The Style Sheets

Next you need to define the styles for the skin. The example shown in Listing 2-11 and Listing 2-12 is a very simple design; feel free to get creative if you want.

Listing 2-11. The Skin's Design Features in public/skins/blues/css/layout.css

```
@CHARSET "ISO-8859-1";

body {
    font-size: 10px;
    background:url(../images/body.jpg) repeat-x;
}

* {
    margin: 0;
    padding: 0;
}

p {
    padding: .5em;
    font-size: 1.2em;
}

#pageWrapper {
    width: 79em;
    margin: 1em auto;
    padding:1em 0;
    -moz-border-radius: 5px;
    border:#749BCE 1px solid;
    background: #fff;

}

#header {
    height: 5em;
    padding:1em 2em;
}

#nav {
    background: url(../images/nav.jpg) repeat-x #FD9421;
    height: 2.5em;
    margin: 0 0 .5em 0;
    padding:.5em 0;
    border-top:#FD9421 1px solid;
}

#sidebar {
    float: right;
    width: 17em;
    height: 40em;
    margin: 0 0 .5em .5em;
    padding: .5em;
}

#main {
```

```
    min-height:30em;
    margin: 0 0 .5em 0;
    padding:2em;
}

#subNav,#adminMenu,#userForm {
    width: 17em;
    height: 10em;
    margin: 0 0 .5em 0;
}

#footer {
    clear: both;
    height: 2.5em;
    margin: 0;
    text-align:center;
    font-style:italic;
}
```

Listing 2-12. The Skin's Typography in public/skins/blues/styles/text.css

```
@CHARSET "ISO-8859-1";

body {
    font-family:Helvetica, Arial, sans-serif;
}
```

Note that you will be doing a lot more work to this skin as the site progresses, but this should make things look a little nicer for now.

Building a View Helper to Render the Skin

The placeholders I mentioned earlier are good examples of Zend_View helpers. The placeholders are one example of the initial helpers that ship with the framework. When these do not suit your needs, it is very easy to create your own helper classes to add reusable custom functionality to your view scripts.

Now you'll create the new view helper class that will load the skin, but first I'll go over a few key points about writing helpers:

- *Filename*: The file's name should be the same as your class name (not including the prefix).

- *Class prefix*: Zend's prefix for the class name is Zend_View_Helper. You can set yours to be whatever you want when you add the path to the helpers.

- *Loading helpers*: The framework will automatically load the helpers located in the current module's views/helpers folder. Those should use the Zend_View_Helper prefix.

- *Class methods*: Your class can have as many methods as required, but it must have a constructor that is named the same as your class name, using the camelCase convention.

- *Zend_View_Helper_Abstract:* Your class should extend the
  Zend_View_Helper_Abstract base class.

First, to create the loadSkin() view helper, you need to create the class. Add a new file to application/views/helpers named LoadSkin.php. Next, open this file, and add the class for your helper. The class name should be Zend_View_Helper_LoadSkin, and it should extend Zend_View_Helper_Abstract.

Then create the constructor method, loadSkin(), which you need to be able to pass the skin that you want to load to. The helper will load the config file for this skin and then add each of the style sheets that are specified to the view headLink() placeholder, as shown in Listing 2-13.

Listing 2-13. The loadSkin() Class in application/views/helpers/LoadSkin.php

```php
<?php
/**
 * this class loads the cms skin
 *
 */
class Zend_View_Helper_LoadSkin extends Zend_View_Helper_Abstract
{
    public function loadSkin ($skin)
    {
        // load the skin config file
        $skinData = new Zend_Config_Xml('./skins/' . $skin . '/skin.xml');
        $stylesheets = $skinData->stylesheets->stylesheet->toArray();
        // append each stylesheet
        if (is_array($stylesheets)) {
            foreach ($stylesheets as $stylesheet) {
                $this->view->headLink()->appendStylesheet('/skins/' . $skin .
                    '/css/' . $stylesheet);
            }
        }
    }
}
```

Using the loadSkin Helper

The loadSkin helper requires that you pass it a valid skin. You could set this skin setting in the layout script when you call the helper, but this can make your CMS less flexible; ideally, you should be able to switch the skins without touching the layout file.

You may want to do something more dynamic in the future, but for now it makes sense to set the skin while you are bootstrapping the application. As I mentioned in the first chapter, Zend_Application initializes the front controller by default, which in turn initializes Zend_View. This default behavior is sufficient most of the time, but in this case you need more control over the process. To get this control, you can initialize the view yourself and then set the view object manually.

The first thing you need to do is create a new method in the Bootstrap class called _initView() (Listing 2-14). In the _initView() method, you will create a new instance of Zend_View. Then you need to set the doctype and page title. Next set the skin to the blues skin. Once this is set, you fetch the ViewRenderer action helper and manually set this instance as the view instance for it to use.

Listing 2-14. The _initView() Method in application/Bootstrap.php

```
protected function _initView()
{
    // Initialize view
    $view = new Zend_View();
    $view->doctype('XHTML1_STRICT');
    $view->headTitle('Zend CMS');
    $view->skin = 'blues';

    // Add it to the ViewRenderer
    $viewRenderer = Zend_Controller_Action_HelperBroker::getStaticHelper(
        'ViewRenderer'
    );
    $viewRenderer->setView($view);

    // Return it, so that it can be stored by the bootstrap
    return $view;
}
```

Now that the view is set, you need to update the layout script to use the skin. Replace the line in the head of your layout script that appended the layout.css file with a call to the loadSkin() helper. You need to pass this the skin that you set in the Bootstrap file, as in Listing 2-15.

Listing 2-15. Updating the Layout Script to Use the loadSkin() Helper

application/layouts/scripts/layout.phtml

```
$this->loadSkin($this->skin);
```

Testing the Skin

Now that the skin is implemented, it's time to admire your work. Navigate to http://localhost. The layout should now use your skin and be a little easier on the eyes (see Figure 2-6).

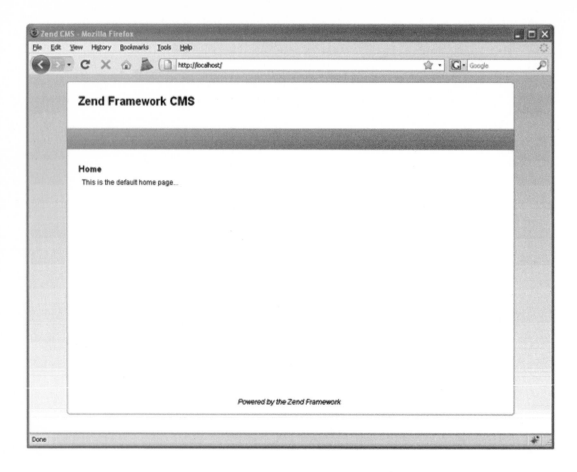

Figure 2-6. The completed template with the new skin

Summary

In this chapter, you learned how to create and manage designs using Zend Framework's presentation layer. Then you created the default site skin, which will be used throughout the rest of the book.

CHAPTER 3

■ ■ ■

Building and Processing Web Forms with Zend_Form

Almost every aspect of your CMS project will be dealing with dynamic data in one form or another. Managing this data is broken down into two areas of responsibility:

- *Capturing the data*: The data is captured, validated, and filtered by Zend_Form.

- *Storing the data*: This depends on the data source, but in the case of this CMS, the data will be stored by Zend_Db.

This separation contrasts some other patterns that handle data validation and filtering in the database abstraction layer. There is a good reason for this; a database is only one of many data sources that are at an application developer's disposal. It is common to use several sources in the same application. When the form object handles this, you can send the data to any source with confidence.

The Anatomy of a Zend Framework Form

Zend_Form is easy to visualize if you consider how an actual XHTML form is constructed. An XHTML form is wrapped in the <form /> element, which can have a number of attributes, such as method, action, id, and so on. Once you have this form element defined, you add elements to it for each of the different controls. These controls can have a number of attributes as well, such as the type, name, value, and so on. Beyond these standard HTML control attributes, you can also add multiple validators and filters to each of the controls.

■ **Note** In this section I am explaining how to work with Zend_Form_Elements. Zend Framework also provides several view helpers that generate HTML controls. The main difference between these two is the fact that Zend_Form_Elements are objects that are part of a Zend_Form, while the helpers simply generate the HTML controls.

A Zend_Form-based form works in the same way. The Zend_Form object serves as a container for Zend_Form_Element objects, and it has all of the standard form attributes. There are Zend_Form_Element objects for each of the standard web form controls, and each of these controls has the standard XHTML attributes. Zend_Form also supports several non-standard form controls, such as Dojo widgets.

Rendering Forms

The principal difference between Zend_Form and an XHTML form is the fact that Zend_Form is a PHP object that represents the XHTML form. To render the form, you use the Zend_Form instance's render() method, which returns the markup for the form.

The actual process of converting this object to the XHTML output is handled by *decorators*. These decorators are snippets of code that render the appropriate markup dynamically. You have complete control over which decorators are used to render each of the components.

Processing a Form

Once the form has been completed and submitted, the form object switches gears and processes the data. First you confirm that the data is valid by passing an array of the data to the isValid() method to validate. If the data passes the validation test, you retrieve the validated and filtered data from the form using the getValues() method, as in the example in Listing 3-1.

Listing 3-1. Processing a Zend_Form

```php
<?php
$form = new Zend_Form();
// add some elements to the form
$data = $_POST; // this data can be any array
// validate the form
if($form->isValid($data)) {
    // if the form passes the validation test fetch the values
    // these values will be returned as an array of validated and filtered data
    $cleanData = $form->getValues();
}
```

Form Elements

Form elements are classes that represent HTML controls. These classes handle rendering the controls with the appropriate metadata and attributes and then validating and filtering the data.

Initial Elements

Zend_Form includes a number of commonly used form elements in the base framework, described in the following sections.

Zend_Form_Element_Button

The Button control creates an HTML button element. You can check to see whether the button was clicked by using the isChecked() method.

Zend_Form_Element_Captcha

Captcha is used to confirm that a human is submitting a form. A number of Captcha adapters are included in the framework.

Zend_Form_Element_Checkbox

The checkbox element creates an HTML check box. If the check box is selected, then its value will be posted. Otherwise, nothing will be posted. You can also use the isChecked() method to test it explicitly.

Zend_Form_Element_File

The file element creates an HTML file upload control. This control uses Zend_File_Transfer to add the upload functionality to your form.

Zend_Form_Element_Hidden

The hidden element creates an HTML hidden form control.

Zend_Form_Element_Hash

The hash element validates that the current user submitted a form by setting and checking the session.

Zend_Form_Element_Image

Images can be used as form controls using the image element.

Zend_Form_Element_MultiCheckbox

The multiCheckbox element creates a group of check boxes. It extends the multi element, which enables you to specify multiple items and then validate this list.

Zend_Form_Element_Multiselect

The multiselect element extends the select element, adding the ability to select multiple items. It extends the multi element, so you have access to an array of methods to set and get the element options.

Zend_Form_Element_Password

The password element creates an HTML password control. This is essentially the same as a text box, but the value is obscured while it is typed.

Zend_Form_Element_Radio

The `radio` element generates a radio group that displays multiple options, but it allows the user to select only one. It extends the `multi` element.

Zend_Form_Element_Reset

The `reset` element creates a reset button. This button resets the form to its initial state.

Zend_Form_Element_Select

The `select` element creates an HTML select control. It extends the `multi` base element, which enables you to specify multiple options.

Zend_Form_Element_Submit

The `submit` element creates an HTML submit button. If you have several submit buttons on one form, you can determine whether a given submit button was clicked using the `isChecked()` method.

Zend_Form_Element_Text

The `text` element creates an HTML text control. It is the most common form control.

Zend_Form_Element_Textarea

The `textarea` element creates an HTML text area control. The text area control enables the user to enter large quantities of text.

Custom Form Elements

You can create custom form elements to reuse your controls. A base `Zend_Form_Element` can be extended to add custom functionality, validators, filters, and decorators to your form element as necessary.

Creating a Page Form

Bugs are an unfortunate but inevitable part of application development. This is especially true during the early iterations of a component that is developed with the Agile and RAD development methodologies. How you manage these issues plays a large role in the overall efficiency of your development process.

This makes a bug manager a very useful example to demonstrate how you manage data with Zend Framework. In this chapter, you will create and render a bug report form.

Getting Started

The first thing you need to do to get started adding any functionality to a ZF application is to create an action and the associated view. In this case, you are adding new functionality, rather than adding to an existing function, so you will need to create a new controller for the action.

Zend_Tool makes adding these controllers and actions a straightforward process. Note that although I use Zend_Tool, you can also create these files and classes manually in your favorite text editor. Open your command-line tool, and navigate to the root of your project. Then use the `create controller` command to create the new controller and its associated views. You pass this command a single argument, the name of the controller, as in Listing 3-2.

Listing 3-2. The `create controller` Command

```
zf create controller bug
```

Now when you take a look at your project, you should see that this command created the BugController, a folder for its views, and the index action/view script.

Next you need to create the submit action, which will be used to submit new bugs. You do this with the `create action` command. You pass the `create action` command two arguments, namely, the name of the action and the name of the controller, as in Listing 3-3.

Listing 3-3. The `create action` Command

```
zf create action create bug
```

Next take a moment to make sure you set this action up properly. If you point your browser to http://localhost/bug/create, you should see your new page, which should render the default Zend view script. This script simply tells you the controller and action that have been dispatched.

Creating the Form

You can build forms using Zend_Form in a number of ways. You can build them manually in your controllers as needed, create them from Zend_Config objects, or create classes for them. I prefer the third approach for several reasons:

- You can reuse your forms throughout the application.

- By creating a class that extends Zend_Form, you are able to customize the functionality of the core form object.

To get started, create a new folder in application named forms (Listing 3-4).

Listing 3-4. The forms Folder in application

```
/ application
    / forms
```

Next create a new file in the application/forms folder named BugReportForm.php. Create a class in this file named Form_BugReportForm that extends Zend_Form. Note that I added the Form_ namespace to this class, which enables you to load the form resources with Zend_Loader_Autoloader rather than manually including each file (Listing 3-5).

Listing 3-5. The Base Form_BugReportForm Class in application/forms/BugReportForm.php

```php
<?php
class Form_BugReportForm extends Zend_Form
{
}
```

Adding Controls to the Form

You can add controls to your form in several ways as well. You can create a form and then add controls to this specific instance, but this method must be duplicated everywhere you use the form. I prefer adding the controls directly to the form class.

Zend_Form calls the init() method when the form class is constructed. This is done so it is easier for developers to add functionality to the constructor without having to manually call the parent::_construct() method. This is where you should add the elements to the form.

The bug report form will need several fields initially: author, e-mail, date, URL, description, priority, and status.

- *Author*: The author field will be a text box that will enable people to enter their names when they submit a bug report. This field is required.

- *E-mail*: The e-mail field will be a text box where the submitter can enter their e-mail address. It is required, and it must be a valid e-mail address.

- *Date*: The date field will be a text box where the user will enter the date on which the issue occurred. It should default to the current day, it is required, and it must be a valid date.

- *URL*: This field will be a text box and is the URL of the site where the issue occurred. It is required.

- *Description*: This control will be a text area and is a description of the issue. It is required.

- *Priority*: This will be a select control, so the user can choose from a list of priority levels. It will default to low.

- *Status*: This will be the current status of the issue. It will be a select control and will default to new.

To get started, create a new method in the Form_BugReportForm form class named init(). In Listing 3-6, I added comments where you will add each of these form controls.

Listing 3-6. The Form_BugReportForm Form init() Function in application/forms/BugReportForm.php

```php
class Form_BugReportForm extends Zend_Form
{
    public function init()
```

```
{
    // add element: author textbox
    // add element: email textbox
    // add element: date textbox
    // add element: URL textbox
    // add element: description text area
    // add element: priority select box
    // add element: status select box
    // add element: submit button
    }
}
```

Now you are ready to start creating the controls. There are two ways to create the controls; you can instantiate a new instance of the form element class, or you can use the Zend_Form instance's createElement() method. In this example, you will use the createElement() method, which takes two arguments: the type and name of the control. It returns the instance of the element you just created.

The Author Text Control

The first control you need to add is the author text box. Create a new element that has the type set to text and author for the name. Then you set the label for the control, set its required flag to true, and set any other attributes you may need. In this case, you should set the size to 30 (Listing 3-7).

Listing 3-7. Creating the Author Text Box in application/forms/BugReportForm.php

```
$author = $this->createElement('text', 'author');
$author->setLabel('Enter your name:');
$author->setRequired(TRUE);
$author->setAttrib('size', 30);
$this->addElement($author);
```

The E-mail Text Control

The next control you need to add is the e-mail field. This control will be a text box like the author but will require more validation and filtering. First you need to validate that the value is in fact a valid e-mail address. Then you will strip any whitespace from the value and convert the whole address to lowercase. You add these filters and validators using the following Zend_Form_Element methods:

- addFilter(): This method adds a single filter.

- addFilters(): This method adds an array of filters.

- addValidator(): This method adds a single validator.

- addValidators(): This method adds an array of validators.

Each of these methods can accept the filter/validator as a string (the class name of the filter/validator) or as an instance of the filter/validator class. This is strictly a matter of preference; I use the latter because Zend Studio's code complete function will give me a list of the available options, as shown in Listing 3-8.

Listing 3-8. Creating the E-mail Text Box in application/forms/BugReportForm.php

```
$email = $this->createElement('text', 'email');
$email->setLabel('Your email address:');
$email->setRequired(TRUE);
$email->addValidator(new Zend_Validate_EmailAddress());
$email->addFilters(array(
    new Zend_Filter_StringTrim(),
    new Zend_Filter_StringToLower()
    ));
$email->setAttrib('size', 40);
$this->addElement($email);
```

The Date Text Control

The date field will be a text box as well. It is required, and it must be a valid date. You can validate the date using the Zend_Validate_Date() validator, which you pass the date format to (see Listing 3-9).

Listing 3-9. Creating the Date Text Box in application/forms/BugReportForm.php

```
$date = $this->createElement('text', 'date');
$date->setLabel('Date the issue occurred (mm-dd-yyyy):');
$date->setRequired(TRUE);
$date->addValidator(new Zend_Validate_Date('MM-DD-YYYY'));
$date->setAttrib('size',20);
$this->addElement($date);
```

The URL Text Control

Next you need to add the field for the URL that the issue occurred on. At the time of writing, there is no URI validator included in Zend_Validate; you must write a custom validator to do this. For this example, just set the field to required, as shown in Listing 3-10.

Listing 3-10. Creating the URL Text Box in application/forms/BugReportForm.php

```
$url = $this->createElement('text', 'url');
$url->setLabel('Issue URL:');
$url->setRequired(TRUE);
$url->setAttrib('size',50);
$this->addElement($url);
```

The Description Text Area Control

The description field will be a text area control. Creating this control is very similar to creating a text field. The only differences are that you pass the createElement() method textarea rather than text and that it has a few different attributes (see Listing 3-11).

Listing 3-11. Creating the Description Text Area in application/forms/BugReportForm.php

```
$description = $this->createElement('textarea', 'description');
$description->setLabel('Issue description:');
$description->setRequired(TRUE);
$description->setAttrib('cols',50);
$description->setAttrib('rows',4);
$this->addElement($description);
```

The Priority Select Control

The priority field will be a select control. Select controls require one more step to create as opposed to text and text area controls; you must add the options that the user can select. There are two different ways to do this. You can add each option separately, using the addMultiOption() method. Alternatively, you can add an array of options using the addMultiOptions() method, where the key is the value of the option and the value is the label. Use the addMultiOptions() method for the priority field, as shown in Listing 3-12.

Listing 3-12. Creating the Priority Select Control in application/forms/BugReportForm.php

```
$priority = $this->createElement('select', 'priority');
$priority->setLabel('Issue priority:');
$priority->setRequired(TRUE);
$priority->addMultiOptions(array(
    'low'     => 'Low',
    'med'     => 'Medium',
    'high'    => 'High'
));
$this->addElement($priority);
```

The Status Select Control

The status field is a select control as well. For the sake of the example, use the addMultiOption() method for this control, as shown in Listing 3-13.

Listing 3-13. Creating the Status Select Control in application/forms/BugReportForm.php

```
$status = $this->createElement('select', 'status');
$status->setLabel('Current status:');
$status->setRequired(TRUE);
$status->addMultiOption('new', 'New');
$status->addMultiOption('in_progress', 'In Progress');
$status->addMultiOption('resolved', 'Resolved');
$this->addElement($status);
```

The Submit Button

Finally, you need to add a submit button to the form. The submit button is one of the simplest controls, so I usually add it directly to the form instead of creating an instance, configuring it, and then adding it, as shown in Listing 3-14.

Listing 3-14. Creating the Submit Control in application/forms/BugReportForm.php

```
$this->addElement('submit', 'submit', array('label' => 'Submit'));
```

Rendering the Form

Now that you have created the bug report form, you are ready to add it to the bug submission page.

The first thing you need to do is update the Bootstrap class to configure the autoloader, adding the Form_ namespace so it can load the form classes for you. The default Zend_Loader will load all the library classes that follow the Zend library naming convention, but there are instances where the class name does not necessarily map to the directory. Zend_Loader_Autoloader_Resource enables you to specify additional namespaces (such as the Form_ namespace) and where they map.

To get started, add a new init method to the Bootstrap class named _initAutoload(). Zend_Loader_Autoloader implements the Singleton pattern, so you fetch the current instance rather than creating a new one. Pass the autoloader to the Bootstrap class, then create a new Zend_Loader_Autoloader_Resource for the Form_ namespace, as shown in Listing 3-15.

Listing 3-15. Bootstrapping the Autoloader in application/Bootstrap.php

```
protected function _initAutoload()
{
    // Add autoloader empty namespace
    $autoLoader = Zend_Loader_Autoloader::getInstance();
    $resourceLoader = new Zend_Loader_Autoloader_Resource(array(
        'basePath'      => APPLICATION_PATH,
        'namespace'     => '',
        'resourceTypes' => array(
            'form' => array(
                'path'      => 'forms/',
                'namespace' => 'Form_',
            )
        ),
    ));
    // Return it so that it can be stored by the bootstrap
    return $autoLoader;
}
```

The next step is to create an instance of the form in the BugController submitAction() method. Then you need to configure it by setting the method and action. Once this is done, you pass the form to the view to render, as shown in Listing 3-16.

Listing 3-16. Creating an Instance of the Bug Report Form in
application/controllers/BugController.php

```
public function submitAction()
{
    $frmBugReport = new Form_BugReport();
    $frmBugReport->setAction('/bug/submit');
    $frmBugReport->setMethod('post');
    $this->view->form = $frmBugReport;
}
```

Next open the application/views/scripts/bug/submit.phtml view script. You passed the complete form object to the view instance in the submitAction() method of the BugController. Now update the view script to render the form, as shown in Listing 3-17.

Listing 3-17. The Updated Submit Bug Page That Renders the Submission Form in
application/views/scripts/bug/submit.phtml

```
<h2>Submit a bug report</h2>
<p>To submit a new bug report please fill out this form completely:</p>

<?php
echo $this->form->render();
// echo $this->form; does the same thing
?>
```

Now if you point your point your browser to http://localhost/bug/submit, you should see the completed form in its raw form (see Figure 3-1).

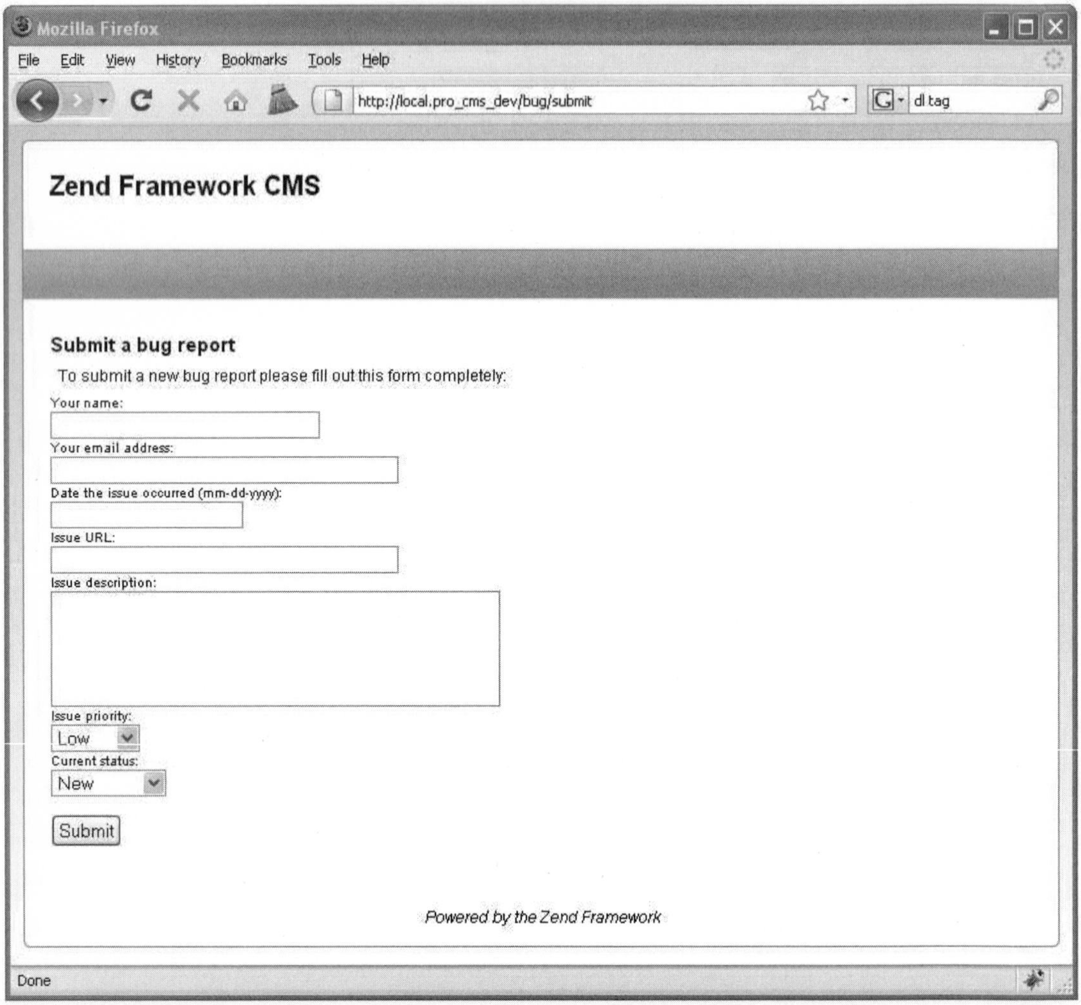

Figure 3-1. The completed bug report form

Processing the Form

Now that your form is created and rendering, you are ready to process it. When you added the form to the controller, you set the form action to the submit action of the bug controller.

You now need to update this controller to evaluate whether the request is a postback and process the form if it is. Zend_Controller_Request_Http, which is the default request object, has a number of convenience methods for determining the request method. In this case, since the form method is POST, you will use the isPost() method to see whether the form is being posted back.

If the form is being posted back, you use the Zend_Form isValid() method, passing it the $_POST array. If it is valid, then you will get the validated and filtered values from the form and simply print them out for now. In the next chapter, you will set up the site's database and then update this controller action to save the bug report in a table, as shown in Listing 3-18.

Listing 3-18. The Updated Aubmit Action in application/controllers/BugController.php

```
public function submitAction ()
{
    $bugReportForm = new Form_BugReportForm();
    $bugReportForm->setAction('/bug/submit');
    $bugReportForm->setMethod('post');
    if ($this->getRequest()->isPost()) {
        if ($bugReportForm->isValid($_POST)) {
            // just dump the data for now
            $data = $bugReportForm->getValues();
            // process the data
        }
    }
    $this->view->form = $bugReportForm;
}
```

Now when you submit the bug report form, one of two things will happen:

- If you entered all the information properly, then submitAction() will print the array of data.

- If there are validation errors, it will render the form again with the appropriate error messages.

Styling the Form

The default browser format for an unstyled Zend_Form is readable, but it leaves room for improvement. A few things that you will likely notice are the following:

- There is no space between the form rows.

- There is no indication that a form element is required.

- If an element fails validation, the errors are rendered as an unordered list, but they do not stand out.

These issues are actually by design; the framework's philosophy is to render usable markup and pass the design control to the developer. To get started styling the form, intentionally leave the name field blank. Submit the form, and inspect the name field (see Figure 3-2).

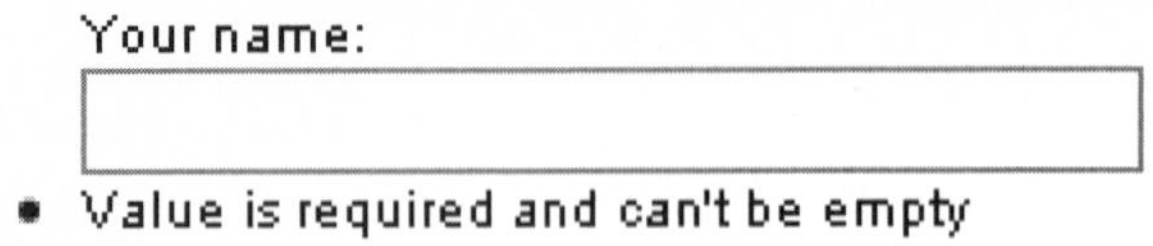

Your name:

• Value is required and can't be empty

Figure 3-2. *The unstyled name field*

Now inspect the markup that has been generated (see Listing 3-19).

Listing 3-19. *The Name Element's Markup*

```
<dt>
    <label for="author" class="required">Your name:</label>
</dt>
<dd>
    <input name="author" id="author" value="" size="30" type="text" />
    <ul class="errors">
        <li>Value is required and can't be empty</li>
    </ul>
</dd>
```

You will note that several classes have been added to the markup that will make it easier to make your required fields and errors stand out on the page. The default decorator adds the class required to the label of required form controls. Then the errors are rendered in an unordered list, which has the class of errors.

To get started styling the form, create a new CSS file in public/skins/blues/css named form.css.

The first thing you need to work on is the general layout of the form. Add padding to the <dt> and <dd> elements to separate the form rows. Then make the label bold and the text 12 pixels.

Next you need to work on distinguishing the required fields. You can do this in many ways, but a red asterisk is a common mark. You can prepend this to all the required labels using the CSS pseudo-selector before. Then add padding to the errors <ul>, and make the items red so they stand out, as shown in Listing 3-20.

Listing 3-20. *The Form Styles in public/skins/blues/css/form.css*

```
@CHARSET "ISO-8859-1";

dt {
    padding: 0 0 5px 0;
}

dd {
    padding: 0 0 10px 10px;
}

dt label {
    font-weight: bold;
    font-size: 12px;
}
```

```
dt label.required:before {
    content: "* ";
    color: #ff0000;
}

ul.errors {
    padding: 5px 0 5px 25px;
    color: #ff0000;
}
```

Now that your form styles are set up, you need to include this CSS file in your skin. Open public/skins/blues/skin.xml, and add the form.css style sheet to the <stylesheet> section (see Listing 3-21).

Listing 3-21. Adding the form.css Style Sheet to public/skins/blues/skin.xml

```
<stylesheet>form.css</stylesheet>
```

Your form should start to look better and be more usable now. The controls are more clearly separated, the required fields are marked with a red asterisk, and the errors are red to stand out more (see Figure 3-3).

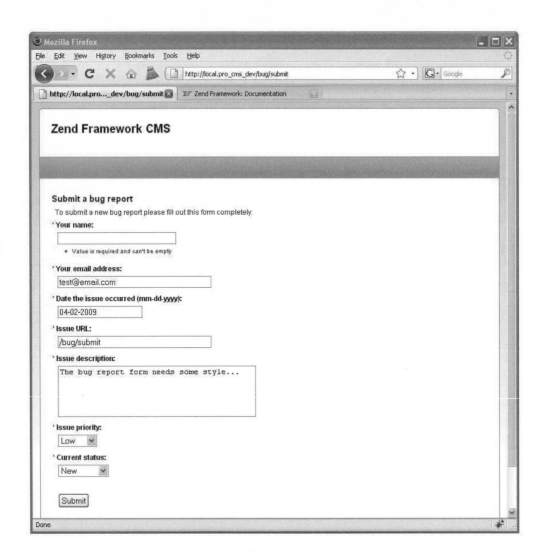

Figure 3-3. *The styled error submission form*

Summary

In this chapter, you learned about working with the Zend_Form component. First, you reviewed what the Zend_Form component is. Then, you learned more about the specific parts of forms and how they work. Finally, you created an actual example that enables users to submit bug reports.

■ ■ ■

CHAPTER 4

Managing Data with Zend Framework

Current web applications utilize a wide range of data sources, including flat files, web services, feeds, and databases. Content management systems exist that are based on each of these sources, or combinations of them, but most of them store their content in databases.

The CMS you are developing in this book will use a MySQL database. What MySQL lacks in enterprise features is more than made up for by its simplicity and speed. The vast majority of LAMP[1] hosting packages include at least one MySQL database.

In this chapter, you will learn how to interact with databases using Zend Framework's database abstraction layer, Zend_Db. Zend_Db is an object-oriented interface to SQL database systems. You will add onto the example you created in the previous chapter, saving the bug reports that the previous demo's form submits.

Setting Up the Database

Before you can start working with the database demos, you need to create the CMS database and configure its connection.

Creating the CMS Database

First you need to create your database. So, create a new database named zf_cms on your testing server, and create a user who has access to this database. This user will need to have permission to select, insert, update, and delete data from the database.

Configuring the Database Connection

Next you need to configure your application's database connection. Zend Framework uses adapters to connect to database servers. These adapters provide a standardized interface to a range of commercially available database systems, including the following:

---

[1] LAMP is Linux, Apache, MySQL, and Perl/PHP/Python. See
http://en.wikipedia.org/wiki/LAMP_(software_bundle).

- IBM DB2
- MySQL
- Microsoft SQL Server
- Oracle
- PostgreSQL
- SQLite

This common interface makes it easy to switch from one back-end database server to another. A common use case is where an application starts with a file-based SQLite database but is scaled up to a full RDBMS, such as MySQL, when necessary.

Zend_Application_Resource_Db is one of the default resource plug-ins that ships with Zend Framework. All you need to do is add the database connection properties to the application.ini configuration file; the resource plug-in creates the connection and then registers it with Zend_Db_Table as the default database connection. Add the database settings to your application.ini file, as shown in Listing 4-1.

Listing 4-1. The Database Connection Information in application/configs/application.ini

```
resources.db.adapter = "pdo_mysql"
resources.db.params.host = "localhost"
resources.db.params.username = "your username"
resources.db.params.password = "your password"
resources.db.params.dbname = "zf_cms"
resources.db.isDefaultTableAdapter = true
```

Creating the bugs Table

In the previous chapter, you created a form for the users to submit bug reports. Now that you have created the database, you need to create a table to store these bug reports in. Table 4-1 describes the bugs table that you'll create.

Table 4-1. The bugs Table Description

Field	Type	Length	Notes
id	int	11	This is the primary key for the table.
author	varchar	250	This is the name of the person who is submitting the bug.
email	varchar	250	This is the email address of the person who is submitting the bug.
date	int	11	This is the timestamp that the bug was reported on.
url	varchar	250	This is the URL the bug occurred on.
description	text	--	This is the description of the bug.
priority	varchar	550	This is how critical the bug is.
status	varchar	50	This is the current status of the bug.

To create this table, run the SQL statement shown in Listing 4-2 on your database.

Listing 4-2. The SQL Statement to Create the bugs Table

```
CREATE TABLE `bugs` (
  `id` int(11) unsigned NOT NULL AUTO_INCREMENT,
  `author` varchar(250) DEFAULT NULL,
  `email` varchar(250) DEFAULT NULL,
  `date` int(11) DEFAULT NULL,
  `url` varchar(250) DEFAULT NULL,
  `description` text,
  `priority` varchar(50) DEFAULT NULL,
  `status` varchar(50) DEFAULT NULL,
  PRIMARY KEY (`id`)
)
```

Exploring the Zend Framework Models

In Zend Framework's MVC implementation, each table in the database has an associated class that manages it. In this CMS we refer to this class as the *model,* but note that a model can mean different things in a different context.

Learning About the Models

The model classes extend the Zend_Db_Table_Abstract class, which provides an object-oriented interface to the database table. It implements the Table Data Gateway pattern; the table data gateway encapsulates all the SQL for managing the underlying table. It provides a number of methods for common database management CRUD (create, read, update, delete) functions:

- *Create*: You can create rows directly with Zend_Db_Table's insert() method, or you can create a new row, add the data to it, and save it.

- *Read*: A number of methods exist for reading data, but the two most common are, first, building a select query using the Zend_Db_Select object and passing this to the Zend_Db_Table fetch methods and, second, fetching a row using its primary key with Zend_Db_Table's find() method.

- *Update*: You can update rows using Zend_Db_Table's update() method, or you can make the changes directly to the row and then use the Zend_Db_Table_Row's save() method.

- *Delete*: You can delete rows by passing a WHERE clause to the Zend_Db_Table's delete() method, or you can delete a row using the Zend_Db_Table_Row's delete() method.

All your application's model classes go in the application/models folder. The classes should use the camelCase naming convention and should use the Model_ namespace. This will enable the Zend_Loader autoloader to find and load your classes for you so you don't have to do this manually. To take advantage of the autoloader functionality, you will need to update the _initAutoload() method in the Bootstrap class, adding the Model_ namespace, similar to the change made for autoloading forms (see Listing 4-3).

Listing 4-3. The Updated _initAutoload() Method in application/Bootstrap.php

```
protected function _initAutoload()
{
    // Add autoloader empty namespace
    $autoLoader = Zend_Loader_Autoloader::getInstance();
    $autoLoader->registerNamespace('CMS_');
    $resourceLoader = new Zend_Loader_Autoloader_Resource(array(
        'basePath'      => APPLICATION_PATH,
        'namespace'     => '',
        'resourceTypes' => array(
            'form' => array(
                'path'      => 'forms/',
                'namespace' => 'Form_',
            ),
            'model' => array(
                'path'      => 'models/',
                'namespace' => 'Model_'
            ),
        ),
    ));
    // Return it so that it can be stored by the bootstrap
    return $autoLoader;
}
```

Creating the Bug Model

Create a new file in the application/models folder named Bug.php. Add a class to this file named Model_Bug, which extends Zend_Db_Table_Abstract. Next you need to define the model's table name; this is not completely necessary, because the framework will default to the class name in lowercase characters, but it adds a degree of flexibility to your class naming. You set the table name using the protected property $_name (see Listing 4-4).

Listing 4-4. The Bug Model in application/models/Bug.php

```php
<?php
class Model_Bug extends Zend_Db_Table_Abstract
{
    protected $_name = 'bugs';
}
?>
```

Working with Bugs

Now that you have the database, bugs table, and model set up, you are ready to start managing bug submissions.

Submitting a New Bug

The first thing you need to do to manage bugs (as is the case with most data) is insert the bugs into the database. There are several approaches to doing this; some people prefer to put the data management logic in the controller action, using the built-in Zend_Db_Table methods. I, on the other hand, prefer to create specific methods in the model classes for each of these actions. It takes an extra moment but makes managing the code much easier down the road.

Creating the createBug() Method

To get started, create a new method in the Bug model named createBug() (see Listing 4-5). Note that you must be careful when naming your methods; make sure you don't overload the core Zend_Db_Table methods!

As I mentioned earlier, there are two ways to create a new row in a table using Zend_Db_Table. I prefer to create a new row object, add the data to it, and then save it. This is a matter of preference, but I find it easier to read and work with than array notation.

Once you have created and saved the row, return the ID of the new row.

Listing 4-5. The createBug() Method in application/models/Bug.php

```php
public function createBug($name, $email,
                $date, $url, $description, $priority, $status)
{
    // create a new row in the bugs table
```

```
        $row = $this->createRow();

        // set the row data
        $row->author = $name;
        $row->email = $email;
        $dateObject = new Zend_Date($date);
        $row->date = $dateObject->get(Zend_Date::TIMESTAMP);
        $row->url = $url;
        $row->description = $description;
        $row->priority = $priority;
        $row->status = $status;

        // save the new row
        $row->save();

        // now fetch the id of the row you just created and return it
        $id = $this->_db->lastInsertId();
        return $id;
}
```

Updating the Bug Controller's Submit Action

Now that you have the database and model set up, you are ready to update the bug controller and implement the submit action. In the previous chapter, you created this action but just had it dump the submitted data out onto the page if the form passed its validation. Now you need to update this action and insert the bug into the database (see Listing 4-6).

First you create a new instance of the Bug model in the submit section. Then, once you have this instance, you call the createBug() method, passing it the values that were submitted with the form. If the createBug() method succeeds, it will return the primary key of the bug row that was just inserted. In this case, you should display a confirmation page (which you will create next).

Listing 4-6. The Updated submitAction() in application/controllers/BugController.php

```
public function submitAction()
{
    $bugReportForm = new Form_BugReportForm();
    $bugReportForm->setAction('/bug/submit');
    $bugReportForm->setMethod('post');
    if($this->getRequest()->isPost()) {
        if($bugReportForm->isValid($_POST)) {
            $bugModel = new Model_Bug();
            // if the form is valid then create the new bug
            $result = $bugModel->createBug(
                $bugReportForm->getValue('author'),
                $bugReportForm->getValue('email'),
                $bugReportForm->getValue('date'),
                $bugReportForm->getValue('url'),
                $bugReportForm->getValue('description'),
                $bugReportForm->getValue('priority'),
                $bugReportForm->getValue('status')
```

```
        );
        // if the createBug method returns a result
        // then the bug was successfully created
        if($result) {
            $this->_forward('confirm');
        }
    }
}
$this->view->form = $bugReportForm;
}
```

Now you need to create the confirmation page. To create this page, you need to create an action as well as a view script. You can do this manually or using Zend_Tool, as shown in Listing 4-7.

Listing 4-7. *Creating the Thank-You Page with Zend_Tool*

```
zf create action confirm bug
```

This command will create a new action in the bug controller named confirmAction() as well as a view script in application/views/scripts/bug/confirmation.phtml. This view script will render a notice with its location and the action that is rendering it. Open this script, and replace this with the thank-you note in Listing 4-8.

Listing 4-8. *The Confirmation View Script in application/views/scripts/bug/confirm.phtml*

```
<h2>Thanks for submitting your bug report!</h2>
<p>We will review it shortly...</p>
```

Viewing All the Current Bugs

Now that you have created a method to enter bug reports, you need to create a method to manage them, which will query the database for all current bugs and create a list view. Each row in the list will represent one row in the bugs table and will have links to update the row as well as delete it.

Creating the fetchBugs() Method

First you need to create a method to fetch the current bugs. You could use the fetchAll() method directly, passing it an array of WHERE clauses, but I recommend using the Zend_Db_Select class. This class is used to create a select query programmatically. Then, once you build the query, you pass the select object to Zend_Db_Table's fetchAll() or fetchRow() method. Zend_Db parses the query, runs it, and builds the result object, which is a set of Zend_Db_Table_Row objects (appropriately called Zend_Db_Table_Rowset).

Create a new method in the Bug model named fetchBugs(), as shown in Listing 4-9. For the time being, you are just going to fetch all the bugs, so all you need to do is get the table's select object and then pass this to the fetchAll() method.

■ **Note** The Zend_Db_Select object is an SQL API that is used to programmatically build queries. There are several advantages of using this API rather than writing SQL. Probably the most important is the fact that the Select object will adapt the SQL depending on the database adapter you are using, which makes the code more portable.

Listing 4-9. The fetchBugs() Method in application/models/Bug.php

```
public function fetchBugs()
{
    $select = $this->select();
    return $this->fetchAll($select);
}
```

Adding the List Action to the Bug Controller

Now that you have a method to fetch all the bugs from the database, you are ready to start working with them. So, create a list action in the bug controller. Use the Zend_Tool line in Listing 4-10 to create the action and view.

Listing 4-10. Creating the List Action with Zend_Tool

```
zf create action list bug
```

Now open the bug controller to update this action. For the time being, this will just create a new instance of the Bug model and pass the results of the fetchBugs() method to the view to render, as shown in Listing 4-11.

Listing 4-11. The listAction() Method in application/controllers/BugController.php

```
public function listAction()
{
    $bugModel = new Model_Bug();
    $this->view->bugs = $bugModel->fetchBugs();
}
```

Creating the List View

To create the list view, open application/views/scripts/bug/list.phtml. This view script will render a table with all the current bugs. To render this table, it will use the partialLoop() view helper, which takes a data set and passes each item in the set to the partial script that you specify (see Listing 4-12).

Listing 4-12. The List View Script in application/views/scripts/bug/list.phtml

```
<h2>Current Bugs</h2>

<table class='spreadsheet' cellspacing='0'>
    <tr>
        <th> </th>
        <th>Date</th>
        <th>Priority</th>
        <th>Status</th>
        <th>URL</th>
        <th>Submitter</th>
        <th>Description</th>
    </tr>
    <?php echo $this->partialLoop('bug/table-row.phtml', $this->bugs); ?>
</table>
```

Now you need to create the `table-row.phtml` view script to render the actual row, as shown in Listing 4-13.

Listing 4-13. The Bug Table Row application/views/scripts/bug/table-row.phtml

```
<tr>
    <td><a href='/bug/edit/id/<?php echo $this->id;?>'>Edit</a> |
        <a href='/bug/delete/id/<?php echo $this->id;?>'>Delete</a></td>
    <td><?php echo date('m/d/y', $this->date); ?></td>
    <td><?php echo $this->priority; ?></td>
    <td><?php echo $this->status; ?></td>
    <td><?php echo $this->url; ?></td>
    <td><?php echo $this->author; ?></td>
    <td><?php echo $this->description; ?></td>
</tr>
```

Next enter a few sample bugs at `http://localhost/bug/submit` to test the functionality, and then go to `http://localhost/bug/list`. You should see a list of all your bugs as a simple table. This table is rather difficult to read, but a little CSS will fix that. Update the `public/skins/blues/css/form.css` file, adding the styles shown in Listing 4-14 for the spreadsheet table.

Listing 4-14. The Style Declarations for the Spreadsheet Table in public/skins/blues/css/form.css

```
table.spreadsheet{
margin:10px 0;
border:#999 1px solid;
}

table.spreadsheet th{
background:#ccc;
font-weight:bold;
font-size:12px;
padding:5px 2px;
```

```
}

table.spreadsheet td{
border-top:#999 1px solid;
padding:5px 2px;
}
```

Now the bug list should be much easier to read, like Figure 4-1.

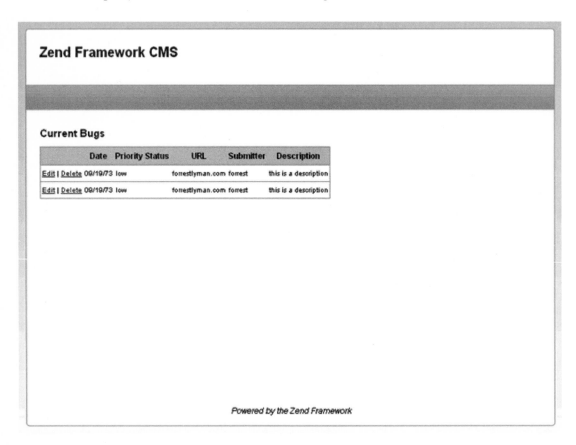

Figure 4-1. *The styled bug list*

Filtering and Sorting the Bug Reports

The bug list is currently renders the bugs in the order they were received. In a real-world example, this would quickly become cumbersome, because you might have to search through hundreds or thousands of bug reports.

Updating the fetchBugs() Method

Next you will update the Bug model's fetchBugs() method to add the ability to filter the reports and sort by different criteria, as shown in Listing 4-15. You will pass the filters as an array, where the key is the bug field and value is the value that you are looking for.

Listing 4-15. The Updated fetchBugs() Method in application/models/Bug.php

```php
public function fetchBugs($filters = array(), $sortField = null, $limit = null,
    $page = 1)
{
    $select = $this->select();
    // add any filters which are set
    if(count($filters) > 0) {
        foreach ($filters as $field => $filter) {
            $select->where($field . ' = ?', $filter);
        }
    }
    // add the sort field is it is set
    if(null != $sortField) {
        $select->order($sortField);
    }
    return $this->fetchAll($select);
}
```

Creating the Form to Filter and Sort the Bugs

Now you need to create a form to filter the bug reports. This form needs to have select controls for each of the available sort criteria and filter fields. It also needs a text control for the filters. Create a new file named BugReportListToolsForm.php in application/forms. Then create the form class named Form_BugReportListToolsForm, adding controls for each of these fields, as shown in Listing 4-16.

Listing 4-16. The List Tools Form in application/forms/BugReportListToolsForm.php

```php
<?php
class Form_BugReportListToolsForm extends Zend_Form
{
    public function init()
    {
        $options = array(
            '0'                 => 'None',
            'priority'          => 'Priority',
            'status'            => 'Status',
            'date'          => 'Date',
            'url'               => 'URL',
            'author'        => 'Submitter'
        );

        $sort = $this->createElement('select', 'sort');
```

```
        $sort->setLabel('Sort Records:');
        $sort->addMultiOptions($options);
        $this->addElement($sort);

        $filterField = $this->createElement('select', 'filter_field');
        $filterField->setLabel('Filter Field:');
        $filterField->addMultiOptions($options);
        $this->addElement($filterField);

        // create new element
        $filter = $this->createElement('text', 'filter');
        // element options
        $filter->setLabel('Filter Value:');
        $filter->setAttrib('size',40);
        // add the element to the form
        $this->addElement($filter);

        // add element: submit button
        $this->addElement('submit', 'submit', array('label' => 'Update List'));
    }
}
?>
```

Loading and Rendering the Filter Form

Now you need to update the listAction() method in the BugController, loading this form and passing it to the view script to render, as shown in Listing 4-17.

Listing 4-17. The Updated listAction() Method in application/controllers/BugController.php

```
public function listAction()
{
    // fetch the current bugs
    $bugModels = new Model_Bug();
    $this->view->bugs = $bugModels->fetchBugs();
    // get the filter form
    $listToolsForm = new Form_BugReportListToolsForm();
    $listToolsForm->setAction('/bug/list');
    $listToolsForm->setMethod('post');
    $this->view->listToolsForm = $listToolsForm;
}
```

Now that you have the form created and loaded, you can add it to the list page. Open the list.phtml file, and render the filter/sort form between the headline and the list table, as shown in Listing 4-18.

Listing 4-18. Adding the Filter/Sort Form to the List View in application/views/scripts/bug/list.phtml

```
<h2>Current Bugs</h2>
<?php echo $this->listToolsForm;?>

<table class='spreadsheet' cellspacing='0'>
    <tr>
        <th> </th>
        <th>Date</th>
        <th>Priority</th>
        <th>Status</th>
        <th>URL</th>
        <th>Submitter</th>
        <th>Description</th>
    </tr>
    <?php echo $this->partialLoop('bug/table-row.phtml', $this->bugs); ?>
</table>
```

Processing the Filters and Sort Criteria

This form posts back to BugController's listAction() method. Open this action. You will need to define the sort and filter variables and set them to default to null. Then check to see whether the request is a postback; if it is, then populate the form, and fetch the sort and filter criteria. Next you need to evaluate whether the filters and sort parameters have been set. If they have, then update the sort and/or filter variables. With this data linked up, you are ready to pass these values into the fetchBugs() method, as shown in Listing 4-19.

Listing 4-19. The listAction() Method in application/controllers/BugController.php

```
public function listAction()
{
    // get the filter form
    $ListToolsForm = new Form_BugReportListToolsForm();
    // set the default values to null
    $sort = null;
    $filter = null;
    // if this request is a postback and is valid, then add the sort
    // filter criteria
    if($this->getRequest()->isPost()) {
        if($listToolsForm->isValid($_POST)) {
            $sortValue = $listToolsForm->getValue('sort');
            if($sortValue != '0') {
                $sort = $sortValue;
            }
            $filterFieldValue = $listToolsForm->getValue('filter_field');
            if($filterFieldValue != '0') {
                $filter[$filterFieldValue] = $listToolsForm->getValue('filter');
            }
        }
    }
```

```
    // fetch the current bugs
    $bugModel = new Model_Bug();
    $this->view->bugs = $bugModel->fetchBugs($filter, $sort);

    $listToolsForm->setAction('/bug/list');
    $listToolsForm->setMethod('post');
    $this->view->listToolsForm = $listToolsForm;
}
```

Limiting and Paginating Bug Reports Using Zend_Paginator

You can add limit and offset clauses to the Zend_Db_Select object very easily. You set the limit parameter, to which you can pass two arguments: the size of the result set and the offset (see Listing 4-20).

Listing 4-20. Example of Adding LIMIT and OFFSET Clauses to a Select Object

```
$select = $this->select();
$limit = 10;
$offset = 20;
$select->limit($limit, $offset);
```

This is useful when you are programmatically building a query, but Zend Framework provides another tool to make the entire pagination process easier, Zend_Paginator.

The Zend_Paginator component enables you to paginate ranges of data from a variety of sources, such as an array, a DbSelect object, or an iterator. It handles these with adapters. In this case, you would use the DbTableSelect adapter. The DbTableSelect adapter adds the proper LIMIT and OFFSET clauses to the Zend_Db_Table_Select object to fetch the current page of results, reducing the memory consumption that accompanies fetching large result sets. It also dynamically fetches the count of the rows that the Zend_Db_Table_Select object will return. It uses this information to calculate the number of pages and results per page. You will need to do a few things to update your code to use Zend_Paginator, covered next.

Updating the fetchBugs() Method to Return a Zend_Paginator Adapter

The fetchBugs() method that you wrote earlier creates a Zend_Db_Table_Select object, runs the fetchAll() method, and then returns the results. Things work a little differently with the paginator; since Zend_Paginator runs its own queries, you need to update the fetchBugs() method to return an instance of the DbTableSelect adapter. One other thing—since the method is no longer returning bugs, you should rename the method to fetchPaginatorAdapter(). I always like to name a method so it describes what the method will do and what it will return, as shown in Listing 4-21.

Listing 4-21. The Updated and Renamed fetchBugs() Method in application/models/Bug.php

```
public function fetchPaginatorAdapter($filters = array(), $sortField = null)
{
    $select = $this->select();
    // add any filters which are set
```

```
    if(count($filters) > 0) {
        foreach ($filters as $field => $filter) {
            $select->where($field . ' = ?', $filter);
        }
    }
    // add the sort field is it is set
    if(null != $sortField) {
        $select->order($sortField);
    }
    // create a new instance of the paginator adapter and return it
    $adapter = new Zend_Paginator_Adapter_DbTableSelect($select);
    return $adapter;
}
```

Refactoring the Bug Controller listAction() to Load the Paginator

Now you need to refactor the BugController's listAction() one more time to fetch the paginator and pass it to the view. Note that as you develop more with the framework, you will see a pattern emerge where you cycle from the model to the controller to the view, working on all three components simultaneously to build and refactor functionality.

You first need to refactor how the controller is handling the request parameters in listAction(). This is because the sort and filter criteria are going to be appended to the page navigation links, so the controller needs to fetch these regardless of whether the request method is a POST.

Now you need to replace the fetchBugs() method call with fetchPaginatorAdapter(). Once you have this adapter, create a new instance of Zend_Paginator, passing the adapter to its constructor. Then you set the page size, which will be statically set to ten rows, and the page number, which you will set by passing the parameter page. Once the paginator is configured, pass it to the view to render, as shown in Listing 4-22.

Listing 4-22. The Updated listAction() Method in application/controllers/BugController.php

```
public function listAction()
{
    // get the filter form
    $listToolsForm = new Form_BugReportListToolsForm();
    $listToolsForm->setAction('/bug/list');
    $listToolsForm->setMethod('post');
    $this->view->listToolsForm = $listToolsForm;

    // set the sort and filter criteria. you need to update this to use the request,
    // as these values can come in from the form post or a url parameter
    $sort = $this->_request->getParam('sort', null);
    $filterField = $this->_request->getParam('filter_field', null);
    $filterValue = $this->_request->getParam('filter');

    if(!empty($filterField)) {
        $filter[$filterField] = $filterValue;
    }else{
        $filter = null;
    }
```

```
    // now you need to manually set these controls values
    $listToolsForm->getElement('sort')->setValue($sort);
    $listToolsForm->getElement('filter_field')->setValue($filterField);
    $listToolsForm->getElement('filter')->setValue($filterValue);

    // fetch the bug paginator adapter
    $bugModels = new Model_Bug();
    $adapter = $bugModels->fetchPaginatorAdapter($filter, $sort);
    $paginator = new Zend_Paginator($adapter);
    // show 10 bugs per page
    $paginator->setItemCountPerPage(10);
    // get the page number that is passed in the request.
    //if none is set then default to page 1.
    $page = $this->_request->getParam('page', 1);
    $paginator->setCurrentPageNumber($page);
    // pass the paginator to the view to render
    $this->view->paginator = $paginator;

}
```

Rendering the Bug Reports Using the Paginator

Once you have the loaded paginator in the view, you need to add a pagination control to let the user navigate through the pages and then update the table to render the data from the paginator.

First you'll render the pagination control. The Zend Framework developers have gone out of their way to keep things as flexible as possible, so the paginator is not tied into any specific pagination control. You create a control and then set the paginator to use it.

To create a pagination control, you are going to need to create a new partial script. Since you want to be able to reuse this control, it makes sense to put it in a common view folder. Create a new folder named partials in application/views/scripts. Then add a new file to this folder named pagination-control.phtml.

The pagination control will need to do several things. It needs to create previous and next links, which should be disabled if you are at the beginning or end of the page set. It also needs to create a direct link to each page. Each of these links will use the url() helper, appending the page parameter and any request parameters to it, as shown in Listing 4-23.

Listing 4-23. The Pagination Control Partial Script in application/views/scripts/partials/pagination-control.phtml

```
<?php if ($this->pageCount){
    // you need to add each of the request parameters to url
    $params = Zend_Controller_Front::getInstance()->getRequest()->getParams();
    // remove the system parameters
    unset($params['module']);
    unset($params['controller']);
    unset($params['action']);
?>
<div class="paginationControl">
```

```
<!-- Previous page link -->
<?php if (isset($this->previous)){ ?>
  <a href="<?php echo $this->url(array_merge(
      $params, array('page' => $this->previous))); ?>">
    &lt; Previous
  </a> |
<?php } else { ?>
  <span class="disabled">&lt; Previous</span> |
<?php } ?>

<!-- Numbered page links -->
<?php foreach ($this->pagesInRange as $page){ ?>
  <?php if ($page != $this->current){ ?>
    <a href="<?php echo $this->url(array_merge($params,
        array('page' => $page))); ?>">
        <?php echo $page; ?>
    </a> |
  <?php } else { ?>
    <?php echo $page; ?> |
  <?php }}?>

<!-- Next page link -->
<?php if (isset($this->next)){ ?>
  <a href="<?php echo $this->url(
      array_merge($params, array('page' => $this->next))); ?>">
    Next &gt;
  </a>
<?php } else { ?>
  <span class="disabled">Next &gt;</span>
<?php } ?>
</div>
<?php } ?>
```

Now you need to render the control. You render the pagination control using the Zend_View's paginationControl() helper, which takes three arguments: the paginator instance, the control type, and the partial script to render. Render the pagination control between the filter form and the results table, as shown in Listing 4-24.

Listing 4-24. Rendering the Pagination Control in application/views/scripts/bug/list.phtml

```
<?php echo $this->paginationControl($this->paginator,
    'Sliding',
    'partials/pagination-control.phtml'); ?>
```

Now all you need to do is update the partialLoop() method that renders the table rows to use the paginator. Since the paginator is using the DbTableSelect adapter, the data is in the same format. You just pass the paginator to the partialLoop() helper in the place of the result set, as shown in Listing 4-25.

Listing 4-25. *The Updated* `partialLoop` *in* `application/views/scripts/bug/list.phtml`

```php
<?php echo $this->partialLoop('bug/table-row.phtml', $this->paginator); ?>
```

Once you have completed this, add a number of test bugs, and then check out `http://localhost/bug/list`. If everything worked correctly, you should see something like Figure 4-2.

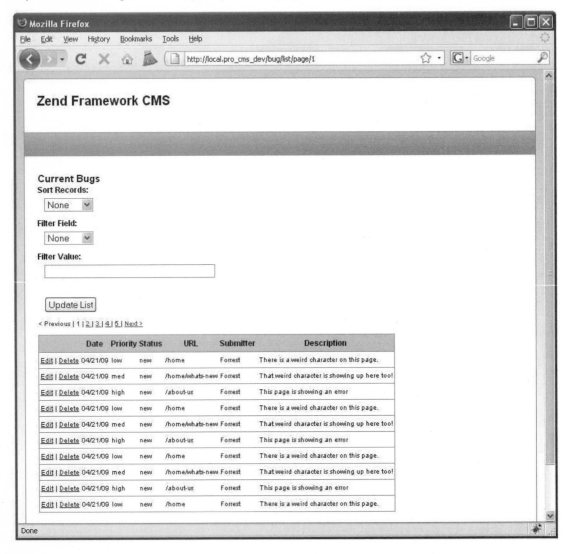

Figure 4-2. *The completed list view*

Updating a Bug

When you created the bug list, you added links to edit and delete bugs. The edit link calls the editAction() method in the bug controller. You need to do a few things to implement this functionality. First, the bug report form does not have any way of identifying the current record, so you need to add a hidden ID field to it. Second, you need to create the edit action and view script to render and process the form.

Updating the Bug Report Form

To add an ID field to the bug report form, open the form, and add the hidden ID control to the beginning of the init() function, as shown in Listing 4-26.

Listing 4-26. The ID Control in application/forms/BugReportForm.php

```
$id = $this->createElement('hidden', 'id');
$this->addElement($id);
```

Creating the Edit Action

Next, to create the editAction() method in the bug controller, first create the action with Zend_Tool, as shown in Listing 4-27.

Listing 4-27. Creating the Bug Controller Edit Action with Zend_Tool

```
zf create  action edit bug
```

The edit action is similar to the submit action, except it needs to open the selected item and then populate the form with its values, as shown in Listing 4-28. Note that Zend_Db_Table_Row has a helpful toArray() method, which makes populating the form with a database row very easy.

Listing 4-28. The editAction() Method in application/controllers/BugController.php

```
public function editAction()
{
    $bugModel = new Model_Bug();
    $bugReportForm = new Form_BugReportForm();
    $bugReportForm->setAction('/bug/edit');
    $bugReportForm->setMethod('post');
    $id = $this->_request->getParam('id');
    $bug = $bugModel->find($id)->current();
    $bugReportForm->populate($bug->toArray());
    //format the date field
    $frmBugReport->getElement('date')->setValue(date('m-d-Y', $bug->date));
    $this->view->bug = $bug;
    $this->view->form = $bugReportForm;
}
```

Creating the Edit View

The edit view script is similar to the submit view script. The only difference is the verbiage; the form handles rendering the different form actions, and so on. Update the edit.phtml file, as shown in Listing 4-29.

Listing 4-29. The Edit View Script in application/views/scripts/bug/edit.phtml

```
<h2>Edit a bug report</h2>
<p>To update this bug report make any changes you need to in this form,
    and then click update.</p>
<?php
echo $this->form->render();
?>
```

Updating the Bug Record

Now you need to create a method in the Bug model to update an existing record. It will be virtually identical to the createBug() method except that you are going to pass the method an ID (the primary key), and it is going to find the row to update rather than creating a new one (see Listing 4-30).

Listing 4-30. The updateBug() Method in application/models/Bug.php

```php
public function updateBug($id, $name, $email, $date, $url,
    $description, $priority, $status)
{
    // find the row that matches the id
    $row = $this->find($id)->current();

    if($row) {
        // set the row data
        $row->author = $name;
        $row->email = $email;
        $d = new Zend_Date($date);
        $row->date = $d->get(Zend_Date::TIMESTAMP);
        $row->url = $url;
        $row->description = $description;
        $row->priority = $priority;
        $row->status = $status;

        // save the updated row
        $row->save();
    return true;
    } else {
        throw new Zend_Exception("Update function failed; could not find row!");
    }
}
```

With this method in place, you simply have to update the editAction() method in the bug controller to call this method on a postback (see Listing 4-31). This will function identically to the submitAction() method.

Listing 4-31. The Updated editAction() Method in application/controllers/BugController.php

```php
public function editAction()
{
    $bugModel = new Model_Bug();
    $bugReportForm = new Form_BugReportForm();
    $bugReportForm->setAction('/bug/edit');
    $bugReportForm->setMethod('post');
    if($this->getRequest()->isPost()) {
        if($bugReportForm->isValid($_POST)) {
            $bugModel = new Model_Bug();
            // if the form is valid then update the bug
            $result = $bugModel->updateBug(
                $bugReportForm->getValue('id'),
                $bugReportForm->getValue('author'),
                $bugReportForm->getValue('email'),
                $bugReportForm->getValue('date'),
                $bugReportForm->getValue('url'),
                $bugReportForm->getValue('description'),
                $bugReportForm->getValue('priority'),
                $bugReportForm->getValue('status')

            );
            return $this->_forward('list');
        }
    } else {
        $id = $this->_request->getParam('id');
        $bug = $bugModel->find($id)->current();
        $bugReportForm->populate($bug->toArray());
        //format the date field
        $bugReportForm->getElement('date')->setValue(date('m-d-Y', $bug->date));
    }
    $this->view->form = $bugReportForm;

}
```

Deleting a Bug

Finally, you need delete bugs. This is probably the easiest part of the CRUD functionality. You simply add a method to the model and an action to the controller. It does not need a view because it will redirect to the list once it has deleted the record.

Adding the Delete Method to the Bug Model

I always create a method in the model to delete records. For a simple example like this, it is not really necessary, but it is a good habit to get into. The reason I always create this method is when you delete items from a relational database, you often have to perform various validation and cleanup tasks. This method gives you a good place to keep them. You also wouldn't want to delete rows outside of the model class for encapsulation reasons.

The deleteBug() method first needs to find the row that is passed to it. If it finds this row, then it needs to delete it. Otherwise, it should throw an exception that the row was not found, as shown in Listing 4-32.

Listing 4-32. The deleteBug() Method in application/models/Bug.php

```php
public function deleteBug($id)
{
    // find the row that matches the id
    $row = $this->find($id)->current();
    if($row) {
        $row->delete();
        return true;
    } else {
        throw new Zend_Exception("Delete function failed; could not find row!");
    }
}
```

Creating the Bug Controller Delete Action

Now create the delete action in the bug controller using Zend_Tool (see Listing 4-33). Since this action does not require a view script, you can delete the script that is generated by the create action command.

Listing 4-33. Creating the Bug Controller's Delete Action with Zend_Tool

```
zf create action delete bug
```

The delete action will be very straightforward. It simply needs to take the ID that was passed to it and call the Bug model's deleteBug() method. Once it deletes the record, it forwards back to the list view, as shown in Listing 4-34.

Listing 4-34. The deleteAction() Method in application/controllers/BugController.php

```php
public function deleteAction()
{
    $bugModel = new Model_Bug();
    $id = $this->_request->getParam('id');
    $bugModel->deleteBug($id);
    return $this->_forward('list');
}
```

Summary

In this chapter, you learned about the basics of data management with Zend Framework and added CRUD functionality to the bug form that you created in the previous chapter. This bug reporting tool served as a simple, real-life example of how Zend Framework handles data; it is not a necessary part of the CMS project, but the skills it introduced are.

CHAPTER 5

■ ■ ■

Working with CMS Data

Your job as a CMS developer is to make managing and publishing information as easy as possible. This challenge is compounded by the fact that the information can take many forms on the Web. There are as many solutions to this problem as there are CMSs, each with its own pros and cons.

One of the real benefits of developing with a framework like Zend Framework is that you don't have to worry about much of the low-level application logic. The framework provides a standardized API, which you can use as you focus on the specific needs of your project. In this chapter, we will follow this model to develop a flexible content management API that the entire CMS will use.

Exploring the Data Structure

How you structure this data plays a large role in how straightforward data management is. There are several approaches, each with its own pros and cons.

Traditional CMS Data Structures

Most traditional content management systems use a fairly standardized data structure that closely parallels the organization of written materials. This structure is broken down into sections and pages, which share some common characteristics, but they are unique entities in the database. Each additional form of content, such as a news article, would have its own table with its own properties.

There are obvious advantages to this approach. The most notable is simplicity. A database that is designed in parallel with the final output data structure is easier and more intuitive to work with. The code is simple and thus less error prone.

The foremost disadvantage is how this structure accommodates changes in the front-end format. Since the database is tightly coupled with the application logic, a simple change on the front end can require updates in every layer of the system. Over the course of time, this can lead to increasingly complex refactoring, which in turn can lead to more bugs. Eventually, such systems will need to be rewritten to accommodate new ways of publishing content.

Abstract Data Structures

Abstract data structures look at content in a different way. In an abstract system, content is content. The database's primary responsibility is to store and serve this content, not to make sense of it. This is solely the application's job.

Let's consider a common example to illustrate how this works. Say your CMS has two modules, one that manages news and one that manages events. On the front end of your site, news articles and events are unique items with unique properties. The key here is to look at the underlying data from another perspective, focusing on what these items have in common.

Looking at Table 5-1, it seems like a good idea to create a common content table that serves both news and events. This would work well initially but does not completely resolve the challenge of building a system that meets your current needs as well as those in the future.

Table 5-1. Comparing News Articles and Events

Field Type	News Article	Event
Text	Headline	Title
Text	Author	Event contact
Text	Teaser	Description
Text	Article	Event
Date	Publish date	Start date
Date	Archive date	End date

Designing a Database That Can Grow with Your System

The preceding example demonstrated that data can be standardized but did not allow for the fact that not all forms of data can fit into this standard structure. Say, for example, that you needed to add a location to the CMS events. Many news articles could use this field, but many would not. In a simple example like this, the problem may not have any practical impact; the articles that don't have a location could simply ignore this field. In a more complex, real-world example, this issue can compound and create more complex issues than the original structure resolves.

The traditional approach to this challenge is to create user-defined fields. A commercial CMS database I recently worked with had one large content table that had several extra fields of each data type: date_1, date_2, text_1, and so on. This solution does allow for future growth but has many serious issues, including:

- What do you do when you need more than two date fields?

- How will the next developer who takes over the project know what the text_2 field is in different contexts?

One solution to this challenge is the node pattern (Figure 5-1). This consists of two components: pages that are the main container and content nodes that are the actual blocks of content. A given page can have any number of content nodes.

■ **Note** You may notice that the *node* pattern, as I refer to it, is very similar to the EAV database pattern. The one difference is the fact that the node pattern uses concrete tables, which can improve performance.

For example, a simple page might have two nodes, the headline and content. A more complicated example might be a blog post that has a headline, teaser, image, and content.

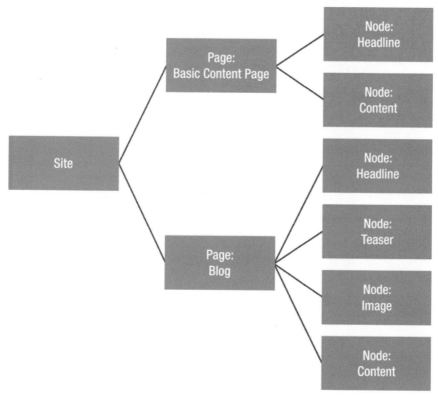

Figure 5-1. *The content node pattern*

The key of this pattern is the fact that since any page can have any number of content nodes, the same database tables can serve the simple page, a blog page, or any other page. The abstract nature of the relationship between the CMS and its underlying data makes it possible to make substantial changes in your site structure without altering the database.

■ **Note** Pages can contain other pages using the structure that we are developing.

Implementing the Data Management System

The data management system is the core of a CMS project. This system will manage all content for the CMS, so it is probably the most important aspect of the project. If you design it well, the CMS will be easy to work with and serve a wide range of needs; if not, you will inevitably be refactoring the system before long.

In the previous section, I went over how to create flexible data systems, focusing on the node pattern, which you will base the system on. Now that you understand the basic principles of the system, you need to determine how these abstract concepts can be used to manage the content of your CMS.

The first step is to decide exactly what information you want to make available in the page object. This data is then broken down into items that are going to be required for every page and items that may be variable. The items that are required by every page are managed by the page component; these include the name and content type. Then the headline, main content, and any other content blocks are managed by the content node component.

Managing Content Nodes

Content nodes are the core content containers, so they are a logical place to start.

Creating the content_nodes Table

The nodes table will be very simple because it will store the content as a list of key-value pairs, with one additional field to make the relationship to the page:

- id: The primary key

- page_id: The foreign key that is used to relate the content node to the page

- node: The key for the content node, such as headline or teaser

- content: The actual content data, usually HTML or text

Let's start by creating this table. Run the SQL script in Listing 5-1 to create a new table named content_nodes.

Listing 5-1. SQL Statement to Create content_nodes Table

```
CREATE TABLE `content_nodes` (
  `id` int(11) NOT NULL auto_increment,
  `page_id` int(11) default NULL,
  `node` varchar(50) default NULL,
  `content` text,
  PRIMARY KEY  (`id`)
) DEFAULT CHARSET=utf8;
```

Creating the ContentNode Model Class

Once this table is created, you need to create the model. First create the file for the model class. Then create a new file in application/models named ContentNode.php. Open this file, and follow the standard Zend model routine of creating a model class that extends Zend_Db_Table_Abstract and then setting the table name property to content_nodes (Listing 5-2).

Listing 5-2. Setting Up the Base ContentNode Model Class in application/models/ContentNode.php

```php
<?php
require_once 'Zend/Db/Table/Abstract.php';
require_once APPLICATION_PATH . '/models/Page.php';

class Model_ContentNode extends Zend_Db_Table_Abstract {
    /**
     * The default table name
     */
    protected $_name = 'content_nodes';
}
?>
```

Creating and Updating Content Nodes

I like to consolidate create and update methods in my model classes; this saves a lot of repetitive coding. It works like this:

1. It will check if whether the page already has this key set; it will use this row if it exists, or it will create a new one if it does not.

2. The row's content is set to the new value.

3. The row is saved.

The advantage of this approach is it makes it easier to use the model. When you need to set a content node, you don't have to repeat the code to determine whether it needs to be created in each of your child classes. Add the setNode() method shown in Listing 5-3 into the ContentNode.php file.

Listing 5-3. The setNode() Method in application/models/ContentNode.php

```php
public function setNode($pageId, $node, $value)
{
    // fetch the row if it exists
    $select = $this->select();
    $select->where("page_id = ?", $pageId);
    $select->where("node = ?", $node);
    $row = $this->fetchRow($select);

    //if it does not then create it
    if(!$row) {
        $row = $this->createRow();
        $row->page_id = $pageId;
        $row->node = $node;
    }

    //set the content
    $row->content = $value;
    $row->save();
}
```

Deleting Nodes

Zend Framework will handle the relationship between nodes and pages. When you define these relationships, you will turn on cascading deletes, so Zend_Db_Table will handle removing nodes when you remove a page.

Managing Pages

The Page model class will serve as a higher-level interface to the CMS pages and their associated content nodes. You will start by creating the pages table.

Creating the pages Table

The pages table will need to store information that every page must have:

- id: This is the primary key.

- namespace: This is the type of page, such as a news article.

- parent_id: This is the parent page.

- name: This is the name of the page.

- date created: This is the date/time the page was created.

To create the pages table, use the SQL script shown in Listing 5-4.

Listing 5-4. SQL Statement to Create the pages Table

```
CREATE TABLE `pages` (
  `id` int(11) NOT NULL auto_increment,
  `parent_id` int(11) default NULL,
  `namespace` varchar(50) default NULL,
  `name` varchar(100) default NULL,
  `date_created` int(11) default NULL,
  PRIMARY KEY  (`id`)
) DEFAULT CHARSET=utf8;
```

Creating the Page Model Class

Once this table is created, you can create the model. First create the file for the page's Model class. Create a new file in application/models named Page.php. Open this file, follow the standard Zend model Model routine of creating a Model class that extends Zend_Db_Table_Abstract, and then set the table name property to pages (Listing 5-5).

Listing 5-5. Setting Up the Base Page Model Class in application/models/Page.php

```
require_once 'Zend/Db/Table/Abstract.php';
require_once APPLICATION_PATH . '/models/ContentNode.php';

class Model_Page extends Zend_Db_Table_Abstract {
    /**
     * The default table name
     */
    protected $_name = 'pages';

}
```

Creating Pages

Next you need to create a method to create a new page. This method will use the Zend_Db_Table instance's createRow() method. Once it creates the row, it will set the row's name, namespace (content type), parent ID, and date it was created. It will return the ID of the page that was just created (Listing 5-6).

Listing 5-6. The createPage() Method in application/models/Page.php

```
public function createPage($name, $namespace, $parentId = 0)
{
    //create the new page
    $row = $this->createRow();
    $row->name = $name;
    $row->namespace = $namespace;
    $row->parent_id = $parentId;
    $row->date_created = time();
    $row->save();
    // now fetch the id of the row you just created and return it
    $id = $this->_db->lastInsertId();
    return $id;
}
```

Updating Existing Pages

Now you need a method to update an existing page. This method will use the Zend_Db_Table instance's find() method to fetch the requested page. If it finds the row, then the first thing it will do is update each of the primary page fields. Once it has done this, it will unset these fields from the data array, leaving the non standard fields that will go in the content node table. Next it will cycle through the rest of the fields in the data array, setting each one as a content node (Listing 5-7).

Listing 5-7. The udpatePage() Method in application/models/ContentNode.php

```php
public function updatePage($id, $data)
{
    // find the page
    $row = $this->find($id)->current();
    if($row) {
        // update each of the columns that are stored in the pages table
        $row->name = $data['name'];
        $row->parent_id = $data['parent_id'];
        $row->save();
        // unset each of the fields that are set in the pages table
        unset($data['id']);
        unset($data['name']);
        unset($data['parent_id']);
        // set each of the other fields in the content_nodes table
        if(count($data) > 0) {
            $mdlContentNode = new Model_ContentNode();
            foreach ($data as $key => $value) {

                $mdlContentNode->setNode($id, $key, $value);
            }
        }
    } else {
        throw new Zend_Exception('Could not open page to update!');
    }
}
```

Deleting a Page

Deleting a page is a simple process. The framework handles the cascading deletes, which will clean up the content_nodes table for you when you delete the parent page (Listing 5-8).

Listing 5-8. The deletePage() Method in application/models/Page.php

```php
public function deletePage($id)
{
    // find the row that matches the id
    $row = $this->find($id)->current();
    if($row) {
        $row->delete();
        return true;
    } else {
        throw new Zend_Exception("Delete function failed; could not find page!");
    }
}
```

Defining and Working with Table Relationships

One of the main factors that distinguishes a relational database from a spreadsheet or other list of data is that the rows in different tables can be related. Zend_Db_Table provides a mechanism to define and work with these relationships.

Defining the Relationships

When you are defining a one-to-many relationship, as in this case where one page has many content nodes, you need to do two things:

- Page model: Tell Zend_Db_Table that the pages table is dependent on the content_nodes table.

- ContentNode model: Tell Zend_Db_Table that the content_nodes table is related to the pages table, setting the columns that relate them, the reference table class (Page in this case), and the reference columns, which are the columns in the reference table.

The ContentNode to Page Relationship

You define the relationship by setting the protected _referenceMap property in the class declaration. In the case of the content_nodes to pages relationship, the content_nodes table's parent_id column is what relates it to the pages table's id column. When you delete a page, you want it to cascade delete all the related content nodes, and when you update the foreign key, you want it to restrict the update.

Add the _referenceMap property directly after the _name property in the ContentNode model, as in Listing 5-9.

Listing 5-9. The content_nodes to Page Reference Map in application/models/ContentNode.php

```
protected $_referenceMap    = array(
    'Page' => array(
        'columns'           => array('page_id'),
        'refTableClass'     => 'Model_Page',
        'refColumns'        => array('id'),
        'onDelete'          => self::CASCADE,
        'onUpdate'          => self::RESTRICT
    )
);
```

The Page to Parent Page Relationship

The Page model has two relationships to control: the page to content_nodes relationship and the page-to-page relationship.

The page to content_nodes relationship is defined by the child table, which is content_nodes in this case. You simply need to tell Zend_Db_Table that the pages table is dependent on the content_nodes table.

The page-to-page relationship is handled by the `parent_id` and `id` fields. You define this using the same technique as you did with the `ContentNode` model.

Add the `dependentTables` and `referenceMap` properties in Listing 5-10 to the top of your Page model, directly below the `$_name` property.

Listing 5-10. The content_nodes to page and Page-to-Page References in application/models/Page.php

```
protected $_dependentTables = array('Model_ContentNode');
protected $_referenceMap    = array(
    'Page' => array(
        'columns'           => array('parent_id'),
        'refTableClass'     => 'Model_Page',
        'refColumns'        => array('id'),
        'onDelete'          => self::CASCADE,
        'onUpdate'          => self::RESTRICT
    )
);
```

Working with Related Items

`Zend_Db_Table_Row` has a number of methods for fetching related records using the references you just set up. These include standard methods, such as `findDependentRowset()`, as well as a set of magic methods; these are methods that are created on the fly.

The following code samples are examples only; you will create the actual methods in the Content Items section, which follows.

To fetch all the content nodes for a given page, you first need to find the page row. Once you have that row, you use the `findDependentRowset()` method, to which you pass the class name of the table you want it to search, as in the example in Listing 5-11.

Listing 5-11. Fetching Dependent Rows

```
$mdlPage = new Model_Page();
$page = $mdlPage->find(1)->current();
$contentNodes = $page->findDependentRowset(' Model_ContentNode');
```

To go the other direction and find a parent row for a given row, you use the `findParentRow()` method. You pass this method the class name for the parent table as well, as in Listing 5-12.

Listing 5-12. Fetching Parent Rows

```
$mdlContentNode = new Model_ContentNode();
$node = $mdlContentNode->find(1)->current();
$parentPage = $node->findParentRow(' Model_Page');
```

Cascading Updates and Deletes

Zend_Db_Table supports cascading write operations, but this is intended only for database systems that do not support referential integrity, such as MySQL. You set these options in the referenceMap and can set either to cascade or to restrict. If you set this to cascade, it will automatically update the child rows. If you set it to restrict, then it will throw an error when you attempt to modify a row with dependencies.

Working with Content Items

The Page and ContentNode model classes provide an *abstraction layer* between your application and the underlying database structure. This makes working with the data much more straightforward, but it still has room for improvement.

The issue is that over the course of creating this flexible data structure, you have made managing the data more complicated than it would be if there were a specific table tailored for each content type. This is a fair trade-off in my opinion, but there is also a way around this complexity. It involves creating another layer of abstraction on top of these models: content item objects. These objects extend a base abstract class that handles all the interaction with the Page and ContentNode models, giving you truly object-oriented data access.

Using the Abstract CMS Content_Item Class

The abstract content item class serves as the base for all the content items that you will create. It adds all the standard functions that the content items need; for example, the methods for loading content items, saving changes, fetching related items, and so on.

To get started, create a new folder in the library/CMS folder named Content and then another folder in Content named Item. Then create a new file in this folder named Abstract.php.

Creating the Base Class

Create a new class in this file named CMS_Content_Item_Abstract. Since this class wraps a standard page, you need to add properties for each of the pages table's columns to it. Make all the fields except namespace public. The namespace field will be set on an item level and should be protected so only child classes can change it. Also, add a protected property for the Page model, which will be loaded in the constructor, so it needs to get loaded only once.

Once you set these up, add the constructor. This should create a new instance of the Page model and set the pageModel property. Then it should load the page if a page ID has been passed to it. Use the loadPageObject() method, which you will create shortly (Listing 5-13).

Listing 5-13. The Base CMS_Content_Item_Abstract Class in library/CMS/Content/Item/Abstract.php

```php
<?php
abstract class CMS_Content_Item_Abstract
{
    public $id;
    public $name;
    public $parent_id = 0;
```

```
    protected $_namespace = 'page';
    protected $_pageModel;

    public function __construct($pageId = null)
    {
        $this->_pageModel = new Page();
        if(null != $pageId) {
            $this->loadPageObject(intval($pageId));
        }
    }
}
?>
```

Loading Pages

You now need to set up the method to load the content items. This method will fetch the current item's (that is, the ID that you passed it) row in the database. If it finds the row, then it needs to validate that the row's namespace field matches the content item's. Then it loads the base properties, which are the properties that you set in this abstract class and are stored in the pages table. Next, the load method needs to fetch the content nodes and attempt to load each of these into class properties. It will do this using a _callSetterMethod() method, which will call a _set method for each node if it exists. This is done so you can manipulate the data that the content item uses.

You will need three additional functions for the loadPageObject() method. It would be possible to simply add this logic to the loadPageObject(), but that undermines the goal of creating reusable code and makes the code less readable. These are the methods you need to create:

- getInnerRow(): This method will fetch the row that the content item relates to from the pages table.

- _getProperties(): This method will return an array of the properties of the content item.

- _callSetterMethod(): This method will attempt to call a setter method for the value you pass it.

The getInnerRow() method is very straightforward; it simply wraps the Zend_Db_Table find() method and sets the content item's *inner row*, which is the underlying data set (Listing 5-14).

Listing 5-14. The getInnerRow() Method in library/CMS/Content/Item/Abstract.php

```
protected function _getInnerRow ($id = null)
{
    if ($id == null) {
        $id = $this->id;
    }
    return $this->_pageModel->find($id)->current();
}
```

The _getProperties()method will utilize several global PHP methods for inspecting classes, including the get_class() method, which returns the class name of an object, and the get_class_vars() method, which returns an array of the properties for a class (Listing 5-15).

Listing 5-15. The _getProperties() Method in library/CMS/Content/Item/Abstract.php

```
protected function _getProperties()
{
    $propertyArray = array();
    $class = new Zend_Reflection_Class($this);
    $properties = $class->getProperties();
    foreach ($properties as $property) {
        if ($property->isPublic()) {
            $propertyArray[] = $property->getName();
        }
    }
    return $propertyArray;
}
```

The _callSetterMethod() will be a little more complex. You first need to establish the naming convention for the setter methods; in this case, I chose to prepend _set to the camelCased content node name, so my_value will get set with _setMyValue, for example. Then you need to check whether the method exists. If it does, you pass it the data set, and if not, you return a message to the calling method. Note that it is considered a best practice to use class constants for any of these messages, so you will need to add a NO_SETTER constant to the head of the class (Listing 5-16 and Listing 5-17).

Listing 5-16. Setting the NO_SETTER Constant in library/CMS/Content/Item/Abstract.php

```
const NO_SETTER = 'setter method does not exist';
```

Listing 5-17. The _callSetterMethod() in library/CMS/Content/Item/Abstract.php

```
protected function _callSetterMethod ($property, $data)
{
    //create the method name
    $method = Zend_Filter::filterStatic($property, 'Word_UnderscoreToCamelCase');
    $methodName = '_set' . $method;
    if (method_exists($this, $methodName)) {
        return $this->$methodName($data);
    } else {
        return self::NO_SETTER;
    }
}
```

Now you have the base methods in place and can load your content items (Listing 5-18).

Listing 5-18. The loadPageObject() Method in library/CMS/Content/Item/Abstract.php

```
public function loadPageObject($id)
{
    $this->id = $id;
    $row = $this->getInnerRow();
    if($row) {
```

```
        if($row->namespace != $this->_namespace) {
            throw new Zend_Exception('Unable to cast page type:' .
                $row->namespace . ' to type:' . $this->_namespace);
        }
        $this->name = $row->name;
        $this->parent_id = $row->parent_id;
        $contentNode = new Model_ContentNode();
        $nodes = $row->findDependentRowset($contentNode);
        if($nodes) {
            $properties = $this->_getProperties();
            foreach ($nodes as $node) {
                $key = $node['node'];
                if(in_array($key, $properties)) {
                    // try to call the setter method
                    $value = $this->_callSetterMethod($key, $nodes);
                    if($value === self::NO_SETTER) {
                        $value = $node['content'];
                    }
                    $this->$key = $value;
                }
            }
        }
    } else {
        throw new Zend_Exception("Unable to load content item");
    }
}
```

Using Utility Methods

Next you need to create the utility methods. These are the methods that will make your life easier when you are working with the items, and you will likely add to them.

Initially, you will need to create a toArray() method. The toArray() method will first get the item's properties. Then it will go through these properties, building an array of the values of the public properties (Listing 5-19).

Listing 5-19. The toArray() Method in library/CMS/Content/Item/Abstract.php

```
public function toArray()
{
    $properties = $this->_getProperties();
    foreach ($properties as $property) {
            $array[$property] = $this->$property;
    }
    return $array;
}
```

Manipulating Data

Now that you have the methods in place for loading and working with the content items, you are ready to create the methods to manipulate the underlying data. You need to create a method to insert a new row, update an existing row, and delete a row.

The insert and updated methods will be consolidated into a save() method for convenience. By doing this, you will be able to create a new instance of the content item, set the values, and then call the save() method, much in the same way that Zend_Db_Table_Row works. The save() method will determine whether the current item is a new item (by checking to see whether the ID is set) and then call the protected _insert() or _update() method appropriately (Listing 5-20).

Listing 5-20. The save() Method in library/CMS/Content/Item/Abstract.php

```
public function save()
{
    if(isset($this->id)) {
        $this->_update();
    } else {
        $this->_insert();
    }
}
```

The _insert() method will call the Page model's createPage() method. Then it will set the current item's ID and call the _update() method (Listing 5-21).

Listing 5-21. The_insert() Method in library/CMS/Content/Item/Abstract.php

```
protected function _insert()
{
    $pageId = $this->_pageModel->createPage(
        $this->name, $this->_namespace, $this->parent_id);
    $this->id = $pageId;
    $this->_update();
}
```

The _update() method will call the item's toArray() method and then pass this to the Page model's updatePage() method (Listing 5-22).

Listing 5-22. The_update() Method in library/CMS/Content/Item/Abstract.php

```
protected function _update()
{
    $data = $this->toArray();
    $this->_pageModel->updatePage($this->id, $data);
}
```

Finally, the delete() method will validate that the current item is an existing row in the database (through the presence of the id field) and call the Page model's deletePage() method if it is (Listing 5-23).

■ **Note** The page model will delete the related content nodes, since you turned cascading deletes on in the page model class.

Listing 5-23. The_delete() Method in library/CMS/Content/Item/Abstract.php

```php
public function delete()
{
    if(isset($this->id)) {
        $this->_pageModel->deletePage($this->id);
    } else {
        throw new Zend_Exception('Unable to delete item; the item is empty!');
    }
}
```

Extending the Base Content Item Class

Now that you have this base content item class, you can create new forms of content for your CMS project very easily, without altering the underlying model or database. You simply create a new class that extends CMS_Content_Item_Abstract and add public properties for each of the data.

For example, say you are creating a module for a tour operator to display their trips. A trip would probably have fields for the title, short description, content, date, length, and cost. You also need to set the namespace, which is how the CMS differentiates between the different page types. So, your content item would look like the code in Listing 5-24.

Listing 5-24. An Example Content Item for Trips

```php
<?php
class Trip extends CMS_Content_Item_Abstract
{
    public $title;
    public $short_description;
    public $content;
    public $date;
    public $length;
    public $cost;
    protected $_namespace = 'trip';
}
?>
```

Then to create a new trip, you simply create a new instance of the trip, set each of the properties as necessary, and call the save() method (Listing 5-25).

Listing 5-25. Creating a New Example Trip

```
$trip = new Trip();
$trip->title = "Long Range Tuna Fishing";
$trip->short_description = "This trip will ...";
$trip->content = "More in depth content ...";
$trip->date = "September 15, 2009";
$trip->length = "15 Days";
$trip->cost = "$2,995";
$trip->save();
```

As you can see, the `CMS_Content_Item_Abstract` class makes working with this data structure totally transparent.

Summary

In this chapter, you reviewed different patterns for CMS data. You then implemented the node pattern. With the database tables complete, you set up the Zend_Db_Table models. Finally, you learned how to create content item objects that abstracts all of this, giving the end developer a very simple interface to the CMS data.

CHAPTER 6

■ ■ ■

Managing Content

Over the course of this book, you have built the foundation for your CMS project. You started by creating the application framework and then added the core models and classes that are required to serve your CMS. Now you are ready to manage content.

Creating and Updating Content Pages

Before you get into coding, you need to define how the page editor interface is going to work. It is common for complex systems to use a dedicated administrator interface. This gives the developers more flexibility. For a straightforward project like this, I recommend the simpler approach of editing pages in place.

The actual content management will be quite simple since you already created the Model_Page and Model_ContentNode classes, which handle the low-level database management, while the higher-level CMS_Content_Item_Abstract class handles the page-level logic.

In this chapter, you will create a new content item class for standard CMS pages (which will extend the abstract CMS_Content_Item_Abstract class). Then you will create the controller and interface for the page section, which will handle the page editing and rendering.

Creating the Page Content Item Class

In the previous chapter, you created an abstract class for the CMS content items, CMS_Content_Item_Abstract. This class handles the required logic to manage the flexible data structure that you implemented with the node pattern. Now you are ready to create a concrete implementation of this class, CMS_Content_Item_Page.

The first thing you need to do is determine which fields you want to have in a standard content page. In this case, there will be two main views for a page: a list view and open view. The list view will render a list of all the pages, with the title, thumbnail, and description. Then the open view will display the complete page. You will need the fields listed in Table 6-1 to manage this.

Table 6-1. The Standard Page Fields

Field	Description
Id	The primary key for the page
Name	The name of the page
Headline	The headline for the page
Image	The path to the page image
Description	A short description of the page
content	The full page content

■ **Note** You will save the page images in /public/images/upload, so create this folder now.

The abstract content item class handles all the CRUD functionality for the content item, so all you need to do is define each of these properties. Note that the base abstract class already has the id, name, and parent_id properties, but I prefer to include them anyway, because it makes the content items more intuitive to read.

Add a new file to the library/CMS/Content/Item folder named Page.php. Define the CMS_Content_Item_Page class in this file (see Listing 6-1), and then set each of the properties listed in Table 6-1.

Listing 6-1. The CMS_Content_Item_Page Class in library/CMS/Content/Item/Page.php

```php
<?php
class CMS_Content_Item_Page extends CMS_Content_Item_Abstract
{
    public $id;
    public $name;
    public $headline;
    public $image;
    public $description;
    public $content;
}
?>
```

Creating the Page Controller

Now you need to create the page controller and its associated view script. You can do this using Zend_Tool by executing the command in Listing 6-2.

Listing 6-2. Creating the Page Controller and Views with Zend_Tool

```
zf create controller page
```

Creating the Page Form

The next step is to create the form that you will use to create and update pages. Create a new file in the application/forms folder named Page.php. Then you need to add a control for each of the page fields. The ID will be a hidden control, while the name and headline can be text controls. The image should be a file control (you will need to set the form's encoding type to multipart/form-data to use this control). Finally, add a text area control for the description and content. Listing 6-3 shows the completed page form.

Listing 6-3. The Page Form in application/forms/PageForm.php

```php
<?php
class Form_PageFormForm extends Zend_Form
{
    public function init()
    {
        $this->setAttrib('enctype', 'multipart/form-data');

        // create new element
        $id = $this->createElement('hidden', 'id');
        // element options
        $id->setDecorators(array('ViewHelper'));
        // add the element to the form
        $this->addElement($id);

        // create new element
        $name = $this->createElement('text', 'name');
        // element options
        $name->setLabel('Page Name: ');
        $name->setRequired(TRUE);
        $name->setAttrib('size',40);
        // add the element to the form
        $this->addElement($name);

        // create new element
        $headline = $this->createElement('text', 'headline');
        // element options
        $headline->setLabel('Headline: ');
        $headline->setRequired(TRUE);
        $headline->setAttrib('size',50);
```

```
    // add the element to the form
    $this->addElement($headline);

    // create new element
    $image = $this->createElement('file', 'image');
    // element options
    $image->setLabel('Image: ');
    $image->setRequired(FALSE);
    // DON'T FORGET TO CREATE THIS FOLDER
    $image->setDestination(APPLICATION_PATH . '/../public/images/upload');
    // ensure only 1 file
    $image->addValidator('Count', false, 1);
    // limit to 100K
    $image->addValidator('Size', false, 102400);
    // only JPEG, PNG, and GIFs
    $image->addValidator('Extension', false, 'jpg,png,gif');
    // add the element to the form
    $this->addElement($image);

    // create new element
    $description = $this->createElement('textarea', 'description');
    // element options
    $description->setLabel('Description: ');
    $description->setRequired(TRUE);
    $description->setAttrib('cols',40);
    $description->setAttrib('rows',4);
    // add the element to the form
    $this->addElement($description);

    // create new element
    $content = $this->createElement('textarea', 'content');
    // element options
    $content->setLabel('Content');
    $content->setRequired(TRUE);
    $content->setAttrib('cols',50);
    $content->setAttrib('rows',12);
    // add the element to the form
    $this->addElement($content);

    $submit = $this->addElement('submit', 'submit', array('label' => 'Submit'));
    }
}
?>
```

Rendering the Page Form

Next you need to create a new action in the page controller to create the new page. You can do this with the Zend_Tool's create action command from your command prompt, as shown in Listing 6-4.

Listing 6-4. Creating the Create Page Action with Zend_Tool

```
zf create action create page
```

Now open the page controller, and locate the newly created createAction() method. Create a new instance of the Form_PageForm() class, and pass this to the view, as shown in Listing 6-5.

Listing 6-5. The Updated createAction() Method in application/controllers/PageController.php

```
public function createAction()
{
    $pageForm = new Form_PageForm();
    $pageForm->setAction('/page/create');
    $this->view->form = $pageForm;
}
```

Now open the view script that Zend_Tool created for the createAction() method (application/views/scripts/page/create.phtml). Add a descriptive headline to the page, and render the form, as shown in Listing 6-6.

Listing 6-6. The Updated Create Page View Script in application/views/scripts/page/create.phtml

```
<h2>Create a new page</h2>
<p>To create a new page complete this form and click submit...</p>
<?php echo $this->form; ?>
```

Now if you point your browser to http://localhost/page/create, you should see the page form, as shown in Figure 6-1. Create a test page, and submit the form.

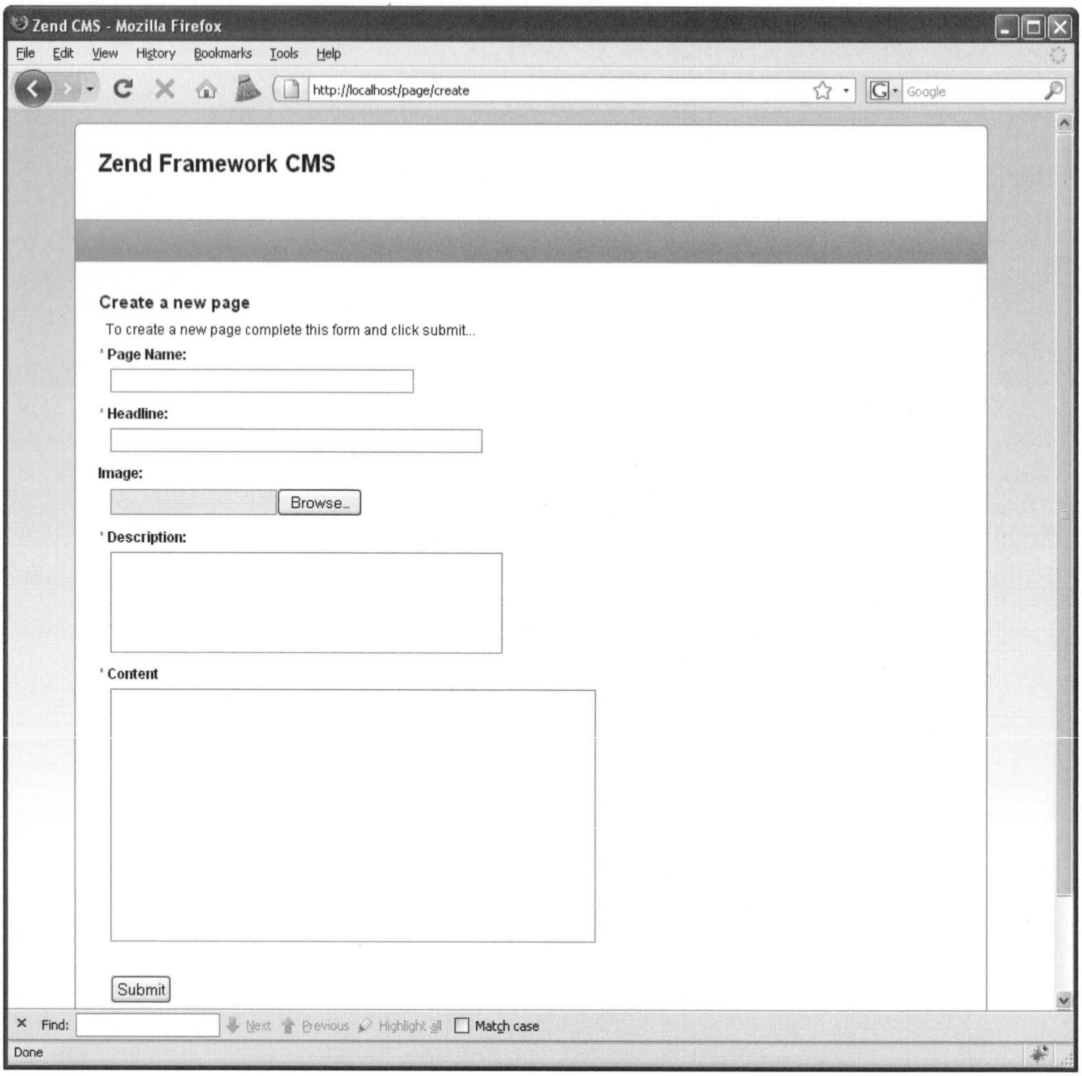

Figure 6-1. The create page form

Inserting the New Page

When you submit the page form, it posts back to the page controller's create action.

You need to update this action to evaluate whether the request is a postback. If it is a postback, then you need to populate the form and validate it. If it passes the validation, then you are ready to create the new page.

To create the page, you need to create a new instance of the CMS_Content_Item_Page class and populate it with the values from the page form. Since you also have one file field, you need to download he file (the page image) and then set the image property in the page object to the path to the image that was uploaded. Listing 6-7 shows the updated createAction() method.

Listing 6-7. The Updated Page Controller createAction() in

application/controllers/PageController.php

```
public function createAction()
{
    $pageForm = new Form_PageForm();
    if($this->getRequest()->isPost()) {
        if($pageForm->isValid($_POST)) {
            // create a new page item
            $itemPage = new CMS_Content_Item_Page();
            $itemPage->name = $pageForm->getValue('name');
            $itemPage->headline = $pageForm->getValue('headline');
            $itemPage->description = $pageForm->getValue('description');
            $itemPage->content = $pageForm->getValue('content');
            // upload the image
            if($pageForm->image->isUploaded()){
                $pageForm->image->receive();
                $itemPage->image = '/images/upload/' .
                    basename($pageForm->image->getFileName());
            }
            // save the content item
            $itemPage->save();
            return $this->_forward('list');
        }
    }
    $pageForm->setAction('/page/create');
    $this->view->form = $pageForm;
}
```

Managing Pages

Now that you have a way to add pages to your site, you need a way to manage them. The first thing you will need to do is create a list of all the current pages. Then you will need to add links to this list to edit and delete these pages.

The first step of this process is to create an action in the page controller to list all the current pages. As your site grows, you may need to allow site administrators to filter and sort this list to make finding a specific page easier, but for now just return a list sorted by the title. Create the list action in the page controller using Zend_Tool, as shown in Listing 6-8.

Listing 6-8. Creating the Page Controller List Action with Zend_Tool

```
zf create action list page
```

Now update the `listAction()` method. Create a new instance of the page model, and then fetch all the current pages. Next pass the record set to the view to render the page list (Listing 6-9).

Listing 6-9. The List Action in application/controllers/PageController.php

```
public function listAction()
{
    $pageModel = new Model_Page();
    // fetch all of the current pages
    $select = $pageModel->select();
    $select->order('name');
    $currentPages = $pageModel->fetchAll($select);
    if($currentPages->count() > 0) {
        $this->view->pages = $currentPages;
    }else{
        $this->view->pages = null;
    }
}
```

Next you need to create the view script to display the list of the pages. This view script will render the pages as a table, using the `partialLoop()` view helper and a partial script to render each row.

Create a new file for the page row partial in the `application/views/scripts/partials` folder named `_page-row.phtml`. This partial needs fields for the page title and for the links to edit or delete each page (Listing 6-10).

Listing 6-10. The Page Table Row Partial in application/views/scripts/partials/_page-row.phtml

```
<tr>
    <td class='links'>
        <a href='/page/edit/id/<?php echo $this->id;?>'>Update</a>
        <a href='/page/delete/id/<?php echo $this->id;?>'>Delete</a>
    </td>
    <td><?php echo $this->name ?></td>
</tr>
```

Now that this partial script is set up, you can create the view script to list the rows. Open `application/views/scripts/page/list.phtml` and set the header as with the other view scripts. Then check to see whether there are any pages, and if there are, create a table to render them. Use the `partialLoop()` helper to render each of the page rows. If there are no pages, then display a message letting the user know that there are no pages currently. You should also add a link to create a new page (Listing 6-11).

Listing 6-11. The List Pages View Script in application/views/scripts/page/list.phtml

```
<h2>Current Pages</h2>
<?php
if($this->pages != null) {
?>
<table class='spreadsheet' cellpadding='0' cellspacing='0'>
    <tr>
```

```
      <th>Links</th>
      <th>Name</th>
   </tr>
   <?php echo $this->partialLoop('partials/_page-row.phtml', $this->pages); ?>
</table>
<?php }else{?>
<p>You do not have any pages yet.</p>
<?php }?>
<p><a href='/page/create'>Create a new page</a></p>
```

You should note that the user row has links to update or delete the user. These links assume that there is an update and a delete action in the user admin controller.

Editing an Existing Page

Now that you can create pages, you need a way to update them. To do this, you need to add a new action to the page controller. You will pass this action the page ID that you want to edit as a request parameter. This action will load the corresponding page and then pass this data to the page form.

Opening a Page to Edit

To get started, you need to create the edit action in the page controller. Create this action using Zend_Tool, as shown in Listing 6-12.

Listing 6-12. Creating the Page Controller's Edit Action Using Zend_Tool

```
zf create action edit page
```

You will use the same form to edit the pages as you did to create the page, which you will populate with the data from the page item. Note that CMS_Content_Item has the toArray() method, which converts all of its properties to an array. This was added specifically to make populating forms, which expect an array of data, as easy as possible. Also note that there is no way to preview the page image. You will need to add this functionality. You could update the form, but then you would need to hide this element when you are creating a page. A simpler solution is just to add the image preview element in the editAction() method, as shown in Listing 6-13.

Listing 6-13. The Edit Action in application/default/controllers/PageController.php

```
public function editAction()
{
    $id = $this->_request->getParam('id');
    $itemPage = new CMS_Content_Item_Page($id);
    $pageForm = new Form_PageForm();
    $pageForm->setAction('/page/edit');
    $pageForm->populate($itemPage->toArray());

    // create the image preview
    $imagePreview = $pageForm->createElement('image', 'image_preview');
```

```
    // element options
    $imagePreview->setLabel('Preview Image: ');
    $imagePreview->setAttrib('style', 'width:200px;height:auto;');
    // add the element to the form
    $imagePreview->setOrder(4);
    $imagePreview->setImage($itemPage->image);
    $pageForm->addElement($imagePreview);

    $this->view->form = $pageForm;
}
```

Next you need to update the edit.phtml view script. This script is virtually identical to the create.phtml file, as shown in Listing 6-14.

Listing 6-14. The Edit Page View in application/views/scripts/page/edit.phtml

```
<h2>Update page</h2>
<?php echo $this->form; ?>
```

Updating the Page

Now you need to process the form and update the page. This form will post back to the edit action, as the create action did. You will need to update this action to process the form on the postback. When the form is posted back, you validate the form data and then update the page if it passes the validation (see Listing 6-15).

Listing 6-15. The Updated Edit Action in application/controllers/PageController.php

```
public function editAction()
{
    $id = $this->_request->getParam('id');
    $itemPage = new CMS_Content_Item_Page($id);
    $pageForm = new Form_PageForm();
    $pageForm->setAction('/page/edit');
    if($this->getRequest()->isPost()) {
        if($pageForm->isValid($_POST)) {
            $itemPage->name = $pageForm->getValue('name');
            $itemPage->headline = $pageForm->getValue('headline');
            $itemPage->description = $pageForm->getValue('description');
            $itemPage->content = $pageForm->getValue('content');
            if($pageForm->image->isUploaded()){
                $pageForm->image->receive();
                $itemPage->image = '/images/upload/' .
                    basename($pageForm->image->getFileName());
            }
            // save the content item
            $itemPage->save();
            return $this->_forward('list');
        }
}
```

```
    }
    $pageForm->populate($itemPage->toArray());

    // create the image preview
    $imagePreview = $pageForm->createElement('image', 'image_preview');
    // element options
    $imagePreview->setLabel('Preview Image: ');
    $imagePreview->setAttrib('style', 'width:200px;height:auto;');
    // add the element to the form
    $imagePreview->setOrder(4);
    $imagePreview->setImage($itemPage->image);
    $pageForm->addElement($imagePreview);

    $this->view->form = $pageForm;
}
```

Deleting Pages

The final step in managing pages is to create a method to delete them. This is a very straightforward process since the parent class of the Content model already has a method to delete a page and all of its content nodes. You simply create an action in the page controller to delete the page and then forward to the page list action, as shown in Listing 6-16.

Listing 6-16. The Delete Page Action in application/default/controllers/PageController.php

```
public function deleteAction ()
{
    $id = $this->_request->getParam('id');
    $itemPage = new CMS_Content_Item_Page($id);
    $itemPage->delete();
    return $this->_forward('list');
}
```

Rendering Pages

Now that the tools are in place to create, update, and delete pages, you are ready to start publishing content. You will create two main pages in this section:

- *Index*: This view will display a teaser list of the recently created pages.

- *Open*: This view will open a selected page.

The Home Page

The default page for your CMS will render a list of the most recently added pages, like most blog packages. Each item in the list will have the title of the page (which will link to the page) and the teaser.

Rendering the Most Recent Pages

To get started, create a new method in the Page model to fetch the most recently created pages. This method will need to fetch the pages in the order that they were created. It then needs to cycle through these pages, opening each one. Finally, it should return these pages as an array that you can pass to the view (Listing 6-17).

Listing 6-17. The getRecentPages() Method in application/models/Page.php

```
public function getRecentPages ($count = 10, $namespace = 'page')
{
    $select = $this->select();
    $select->order = 'date_created DESC';
    $select->where('namespace = ?', $namespace);
    $select->limit($count);
    $results = $this->fetchAll($select);
    if ($results->count() > 0) {
        //cycle through the results, opening each page
        $pages = array();
        foreach ($results as $result) {
            $pages[$result->id] = new CMS_Content_Item_Page($result->id);
        }
        return $pages;
    } else {
        return null;
    }
}
```

The three most recent items will be *featured items*. These items will be rendered as blocks with thumbnails and the full description. The remaining recent items will simply be links.

To do this, you need to create a new instance of the page model and fetch the results of the getRecentPages() method. Once you have this array, shift the first three items off the beginning of the array, and pass these to the view as the featured items. Pass the remaining array to the view as the recent pages, as shown in Listing 6-18.

Listing 6-18. The Index Action in application/controllers/PageController.php

```
public function indexAction()
{
    $pageModel = new Model_Page();
    $recentPages = $pageModel->getRecentPages();

    if(is_array($recentPages)) {
        // the 3 most recent items are the featured items
        for($i = 1; $i <= 3; $i++) {
            if(count($recentPages) > 0) {
                $featuredItems[] = array_shift($recentPages);
            }
        }
        $this->view->featuredItems = $featuredItems;
```

```
        if(count($recentPages) > 0) {
            $this->view->recentPages = $recentPages;
        } else {
        $this->view->recentPages = $null;
        }
    }
}
```

Now you need to update the index.phtml view script to render these. The first three items, or featured items, will be rendered as blocks. These blocks will consist of the headline, a thumbnail (which you will just resize with CSS), and the page description. The remaining items will be rendered as a list of links, as shown in Listing 6-19.

Listing 6-19. The Page Index Action View Script in application/views/scripts/page/index.phtml

```
<h2>Featured Content</h2>
<?php
if($this->featuredItems) {
    foreach ($this->featuredItems as $page) {
?>
<div class='featuredItem'>
    <h3><a href='/page/open/id/<?php echo $page->id; ?>'>
        <?php echo $page->headline?></a></h3>
    <img src='<?php echo $page->image;?>' alt='<?php echo $page->headline?>' />
    <p><?php echo $page->description; ?></p>
    <br style='clear:left;' />
</div>
<?php
 }
}

if($this->recentPages) { ?>
<div class='recentPages'>
    <h3>More Pages</h3>
    <ul>
    <?php foreach ($this->recentPages as $page) {?>
    <li><a href='/page/open/id/<?php echo $page->id; ?>'>
        <?php echo $page->headline?></a></li>
    <?php } ?>
    </ul>
</div>
<?php } ?>
```

Now when you point your browser to http://localhost/page, you should see the list with no particular style. Take a moment now to style the featuredItem blocks by updating /public/skins/blues/css/layout.css, as shown in Listing 6-20.

Listing 6-20. Adding the featuredItem Styles to the Blues Skin in /public/skins/blues/css/layout.css

```
.featuredItem{
    padding:5px 10px;
    margin:10px;
    width:420px;
    min-height:100px;
    -moz-border-radius: 5px;
    border:1px solid #749BCE;
}

.featuredItem h3{
    margin-bottom:5px;
}

.featuredItem h3 a{
    color:#000;
    text-decoration:none;
}

.featuredItem h3 a:hover{
    text-decoration:underline;
}

.featuredItem img{
    width:120px;
    height:auto;
    float:left;
    margin:0 10px 10px 0;
}

.featuredItem ul{
    padding:5px 30px;
}
```

Now when you refresh your browser, the featured item blocks should be cleanly laid out with the headline, a thumbnail, and the description, as shown in Figure 6-2.

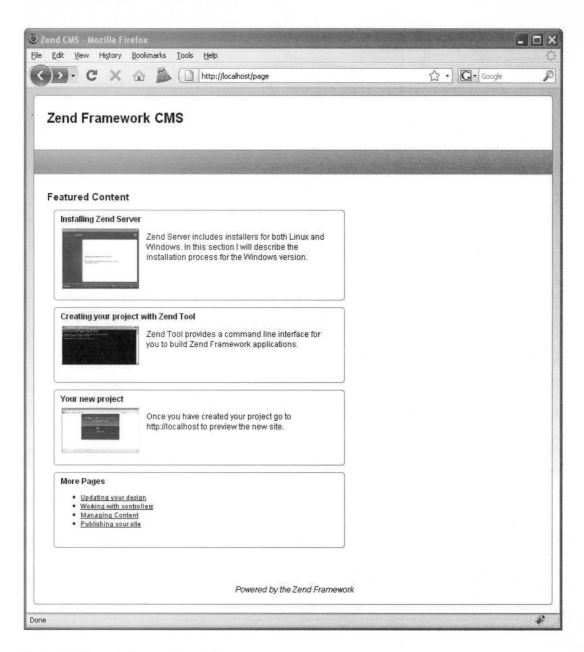

Figure 6-2. The styled featured page list

Setting This Page As Your Site's Home Page

The Zend Framework operates on the principle of setting logical defaults but allows you to override these defaults as needed. By default, the site's home page renders the following:

- *Module*: Default

- *Controller*: Index

- *Action*: Index

The default module and action are OK for this project, but you want to override the default controller to set the previous recent page list as the home page. The Zend_Application's Zend_Application_Resource_Frontcontroller resource makes this very easy to change. You simply have to update the application.ini config file, setting the resources.frontController.defaultControllerName property, as shown in Listing 6-21.

Listing 6-21. Updating the Default Controller in application/configs/application.ini

```
resources.frontController.defaultControllerName = "page"
```

Opening a Page

Now you need to create an action in your page controller to open the pages. Most of the code that you need is already written, so it is a simple process. To get started, create the open action in the page controller using Zend_Tool, as shown in Listing 6-22.

Listing 6-22. Creating the Open Page Action with Zend_Tool

```
zf create action open page
```

The next step is updating the open action. You will pass the open action the ID of the page to open as a URL parameter. The open action will then need to confirm that the page exists. If it does not exist, then it will need to throw an exception, which the error handler will capture. If it does exist, then it will create a new instance of CMS_Content_Item_Page. It will pass the page ID to the CMS_Content_Item_Page, which will in turn load the page data. Then it needs to pass this page object to the view to render, as shown in Listing 6-23.

Listing 6-23. The Open Action in application/controllers/PageController.php

```php
public function openAction()
{
    $id = $this->_request->getParam('id');
    // first confirm the page exists
    $pageModel = new Model_Page();
    if(!$pageModel->find($id)->current()) {
        // the error handler will catch this exception
        throw new Zend_Controller_Action_Exception(
            "The page you requested was not found", 404);
```

```
    }else{
        $this->view->page = new CMS_Content_Item_Page($id);
    }
}
```

Next you need to update the view script, rendering the page content. You can see the completed view script in Listing 6-24. Note that I like to wrap the page with the openPage div. This gives you specific control over the page-level items.

Listing 6-24. The Open Page Script in application/views/scripts/page/open.phtml

```
<div id="openPage">
    <h2><?php echo $this->page->headline?></h2>
    <blockquote><?php echo $this->page->description; ?></blockquote>
    <img id='mainImage' src='<?php echo $this->page->image; ?>'
        alt='<?php echo $this->page->headline?>' />
    <?php echo $this->page->content ?>
</div>
```

Finally, you need to style this page. I will make this very simplistic at this point, simply resizing the main page image, floating it right, and updating the description text (see Listing 6-25). Feel free to get as creative as you like!

Listing 6-25. Adding the Open Page Styles to the Blues Skin in /public/skins/blues/css/layout.css

```
#openPage{
    width:520px;
}

#openPage blockquote{
    padding:10px;
    font-style:italic;
}

#openPage img#mainImage{
    width:320px;
    height:auto;
    margin:0 0 10px 10px;
    float:right;
}
```

Now you have a simple yet functional CMS. If you navigate to http://localhost and click one of the headlines, the page should open and look something like Figure 6-3.

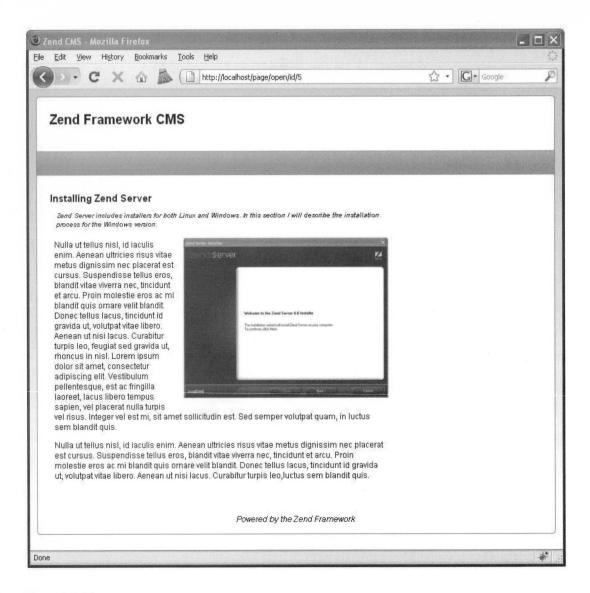

Figure 6-3. The open page

Summary

In this chapter, you learned how to use the abstract data models that you created in the previous chapter to manage your site's standard content pages. You created your CMS page form and then created the functions to create, read, update, and delete content pages. Once this CRUD management was out of the way, you created the list (your default view) and open views for the CMS.

CHAPTER 7

Creating the Site Navigation

Creating a clean design that catches your visitor's attention and writing compelling content are inarguably critical keys of a high-quality website, but without efficient navigation, your site will flounder. The attention span of a typical web surfer is measured in seconds, so if they are not able to find the information they are looking for at a glance, they will almost instantly click away to a competitor's site. When you are developing a CMS, you need to develop tools that make it easy and intuitive for your site managers to build and manage efficient menus.

How CMSs Manage Menus

You have a range of options when managing navigation, ranging from blog systems that automate the entire process following a linear convention that people have learned to low-level CMSs that require you to write custom code to create the menus. Each of these extremes has pros and cons.

The blog approach takes navigation out of the hands of the writer so they do not have to worry about it. This works only for a site that follows the dictated convention, so this approach lacks the flexibility that many sites require.

The low-level CMSs give an experienced developer ultimate control over how the navigation works. The issue with this approach is that it usually requires some expertise to update and manage the navigation.

Like most software solutions, your CMS will be a compromise between these two extremes. It will not automate the menu creation but will make it easy for anyone to add pages to the menus. It will also allow you to add static links to the menu, which will be used to add links to the modules that you develop later in this book as well as the site administration functions.

Managing Menu Data

Every time I build a CMS project, I finish the content management piece and figure that the hard part is behind me, only to be surprised by how much work goes into navigation. Managing navigation is at least as complicated as managing content.

This CMS will use two tables to manage menus:

- menus: This table will contain the menu metadata, which for the time being will just be the name and the access level.

- menu_items: This table will contain the menu items with their labels and links.

To get started, create these two tables using the SQL statements in Listing 7-1 and Listing 7-2.

Listing 7-1. The SQL Statement to Create the menus Table

```
CREATE TABLE menus (
  id int(11) NOT NULL auto_increment,
  name varchar(50) default NULL,
  access_level varchar(50) default NULL,
  PRIMARY KEY  (id)
) AUTO_INCREMENT=1 DEFAULT CHARSET=utf8;
```

Listing 7-2. The SQL Statement to Create the menu_items Table

```
CREATE TABLE menu_items (
  id int(11) NOT NULL auto_increment,
  menu_id int(11) default NULL,
  label varchar(250) default NULL,
  page_id int(11) default NULL,
  link varchar(250) default NULL,
  position int(11) default NULL,
  PRIMARY KEY  (id)
) AUTO_INCREMENT=1 DEFAULT CHARSET=utf8;
```

Next you need to create a model for each of these tables. You will add the methods as you develop this component, so for now, just create the model classes.

The menu to menu item relationship is a straightforward one-to-many relationship, which you can model with Zend_Db_Table_Relationship.

Create two new files in the application/models folder: Menu.php and MenuItem.php. Then define the classes, their associated table names, and the model relationships, as shown in Listing 7-3 and Listing 7-4.

Listing 7-3. The Menu Model Class in application/models/Menu.php

```
<?php
require_once 'Zend/Db/Table/Abstract.php';
class Model_Menu extends Zend_Db_Table_Abstract {
        protected $_name = 'menus';
        protected $_dependentTables = array('Model_MenuItem');
        protected $_referenceMap     = array(
          'Menu' => array(
               'columns'             => array('parent_id'),
               'refTableClass'       => 'Model_Menu',
               'refColumns'          => array('id'),
               'onDelete'            => self::CASCADE,
               'onUpdate'            => self::RESTRICT
          )
    );
}
?>
```

Listing 7-4. The `MenuItem` *Model Class in* `application/models/MenuItem.php`

```php
<?php
require_once 'Zend/Db/Table/Abstract.php';
class Model_MenuItem extends Zend_Db_Table_Abstract {
    protected $_name = 'menu_items';
    protected $_referenceMap    = array(
        'Menu' => array(
            'columns'           => array('menu_id'),
            'refTableClass'     => 'Model_Menu',
            'refColumns'        => array('id'),
            'onDelete'          => self::CASCADE,
            'onUpdate'          => self::RESTRICT
        )
    );

}
?>
```

Now that you have a basis for managing the menu data, you can get started.

Note If you would like more information about how the Zend_Db_Table relationships work, please review chapter 5.

Creating the Menu Controllers

You will need two controllers for the menus, one for each model class. Some people prefer to centralize related components like these into a single controller, but I find it easier to manage if they are one-to-one (one controller for each model/table).

You can create these controllers manually or use Zend_Tool. If you use Zend_Tool, then navigate to the root of your project. Then call the `create controller` command for each of the controllers you need to create. See Listing 7-5 for the complete commands.

Listing 7-5. The Zend_Tool Commands to Create the Menu and Menu Item Controllers

```
zf create controller menu
zf create controller menuitem
```

Zend_Tool creates the controller files and classes (see Listings 7-6 and 7-7), as well as the view folders for these controllers.

Listing 7-6. The Menu Controller in application/controllers/MenuController.php

```php
<?php
class MenuController extends Zend_Controller_Action
{
    public function init()
    {
        /* Initialize action controller here */
    }

    public function indexAction()
    {
        // action body
    }
}
```

Listing 7-7. The Menu Item Controller in application/controllers/MenuitemController.php

```php
<?php
class MenuitemController extends Zend_Controller_Action
{
    public function init()
    {
        /* Initialize action controller here */
    }

    public function indexAction()
    {
        // action body
    }
}
```

Now that the base controllers, tables, and models are set up, you are ready to get started managing the menus.

Creating a New Menu

The menu management will follow the now-familiar routine of stepping through the CRUD process.

Creating the Menu Form

The next step is to create the menu form. The menu form will be very simple; you need only a hidden field for the ID and text field for the menu name. Create a new file in application/forms named Menu.php. Create a new form for the menu, as shown in Listing 7-8.

Listing 7-8. The Menu Form in application/forms/Menu.php

```php
<?php
class Form_Menu extends Zend_Form
{
    public function init()
    {
        $this->setMethod('post');

        // create new element
        $id = $this->createElement('hidden', 'id');
        // element options
        $id->setDecorators(array('ViewHelper'));
        // add the element to the form
        $this->addElement($id);

        // create new element
        $name = $this->createElement('text', 'name');
        // element options
        $name->setLabel('Name: ');
        $name->setRequired(TRUE);
        $name->setAttrib('size',40);
        // strip all tags from the menu name for security purposes
        $name->addFilter('StripTags');
        // add the element to the form
        $this->addElement($name);

        $submit = $this->addElement('submit', 'submit', array('label' => 'Submit'));

    }
}
?>
```

Rendering the Create Menu Form

Now you need to create a new action in the menu controller to create a menu. You can do this with Zend_Tool using the create action command, as shown in Listing 7-9.

Listing 7-9. Creating the Create Menu Action Using Zend_Tool

```
zf create action create menu
```

This will create the createAction() method in the menu controller as well as the view script for this action. Update the createAction() method to create a new instance of the menu form, set its action to create, and pass this to the view (see Listing 7-10).

Listing 7-10. The Updated createAction() Method in application/controllers/MenuController.php

```
public function createAction()
{
    $frmMenu = new Form_Menu();
    $frmMenu->setAction('/menu/create');
    $this->view->form = $frmMenu;
}
```

Now you need to render the form. Open the application/views/scripts/menu/create.phtml file. Add a descriptive headline to the page, and render the form, as shown in Listing 7-11.

Listing 7-11. Rendering the Create Page Form in application/views/scripts/menu/create.phtml

```
<h2>Create a new menu</h2>
<p>To create a new menu complete this form and click submit...</p>
<?php echo $this->form; ?>
```

Now if you point your browser to http://localhost/menu/create, you should see the create menu page. This page should render your menu form, as shown in Figure 7-1.

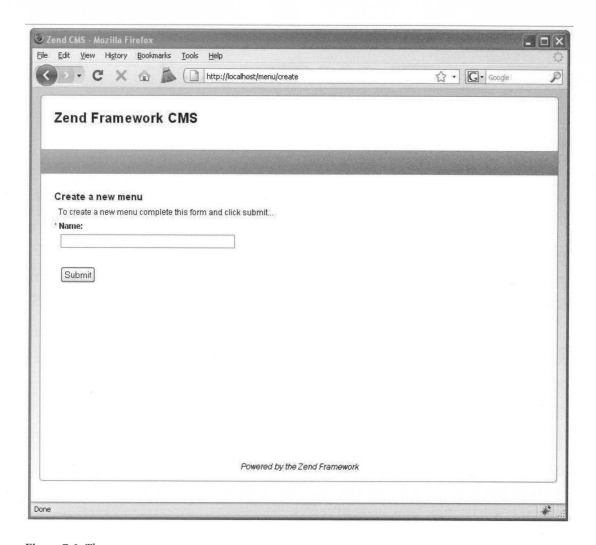

Figure 7-1. *The create menu page*

Processing the Form

Now that the form is set up and rendering, you need to set up the back end to create the new menu. Start by adding a method to the Menu model named createMenu(), which will create a new row in the menu table, set the name, and save it, as shown in Listing 7-12.

Listing 7-12. The createMenu() *Method in application/models/Menu.php*

```php
public function createMenu($name)
{
    $row = $this->createRow();
    $row->name = $name;
    return $row->save();
}
```

With this method created, you are ready to process the form and create the new menu. The create page form will post back to the createAction() method in the MenuController class, so you will need to update this method to create the menu when the request is a postback, as shown in Listing 7-13. You will do this in much the same way as you created pages. If the page request is a postback, then you need to validate the form data. If it is valid, then create the menu. Once the menu is created, you will forward the user to the indexAction() method, which will list all the menus with management links. You will update this method next.

Listing 7-13. The Updated createAction() *in application/controllers/MenuController.php*

```php
public function createAction()
{
    $frmMenu = new Form_Menu();
    if($this->getRequest()->isPost()) {
        if($frmMenu->isValid($_POST)) {
            $menuName = $frmMenu->getValue('name');
            $mdlMenu = new Model_Menu();
            $result = $mdlMenu->createMenu($menuName);
            if($result) {
                // redirect to the index action
                $this->_redirect('/menu/index');
            }
        }
    }
    $frmMenu->setAction('/menu/create');
    $this->view->form = $frmMenu;
}
```

Listing Current Menus

Now that you can create a new menu, you need a way to manage the menus. You will do this by creating a list of the current menus, with links to update the menu, manage the menu items, and delete the menu. Since this will be the main menu management page, you should add this to the indexAction() method. This method will need to fetch all the current menus and then pass them to the view to render.

Before you create the indexAction() method, you will need to create a method in the Menu model to get all the current menus. Add a new method to the Menu model named getMenus(). This method should sort the menus by name and return the Zend_Db_Table_Rowset of the results, as shown in Listing 7-14. Note that I like to evaluate whether there are any results and return null if not.

Listing 7-14. The getMenus() Method in application/models/Menu.php

```
public function getMenus()
{
    $select = $this->select();
    $select->order('name');
    $menus = $this->fetchAll($select);
    if($menus->count() > 0) {
        return $menus;
    }else{
        return null;
    }
}
```

Now update the indexAction() method. This method should create a new instance of the Menu model and pass the results of the getMenus() method to the view to render, as shown in Listing 7-15.

Listing 7-15. The indexAction() in application/controllers/MenuController.php

```
public function indexAction()
{
    $mdlMenu = new Model_Menu();
    $this->view->menus = $mdlMenu->getMenus();
}
```

Next create a new view script in application/views/scripts/menu named index.phtml. Open this view script, and set the page title and headline as usual. Then check to see whether there are any menus currently. If there are menus, then create a table to list them, with a column for the edit, open, and delete linksand a column for the name. Use the partialLoop() helper to render the table rows (you will create the partial in one moment). If there aren't any menus, then just display a message to that effect. You should also add a link on the bottom to add a new menu. You can see the complete view script in Listing 7-16.

Listing 7-16. The Menu Admin List in application/views/scripts/menu/index.phtml

```
<h2>Current Menus</h2>
<?php if($this->menus != null) { ?>
<table class='spreadsheet' cellpadding='0' cellspacing='0'>
    <tr>
        <th>Links</th>
        <th>Menu Name</th>
    </tr>
    <?php echo $this->partialLoop('partials/_menu-row.phtml', $this->menus); ?>
</table>
<?php }else{?>
<p>You do not have any menus yet.</p>
<?php }?>
<p><a href='/menu/create'>Create a new menu</a></p>
```

Now create the partial script to render the menu row. Create a new f file in the partials folder named _menu-row.phtml. This file will render the table row for the menu, with links to edit it, manage its items, and delete it, as shown in Listing 7-17.

Listing 7-17. The Menu Row Partial in application/views/scripts /partials_menu-row.phtml

```
<tr>
    <td class='links'>
        <a href='/menu/edit/id/<?php echo $this->id;?>'>Edit</a> |
        <a href='/menuitem/index/menu/<?php echo $this->id;?>'>
            Manage Menu Items</a> |
        <a href='/menu/delete/id/<?php echo $this->id;?>'>Delete</a>
    </td>
    <td><?php echo $this->name ?></td>
</tr>
```

When you have completed this, you should be able to point your browser to http://localhost/menu and see a list of the menus, as shown in Figure 7-2.

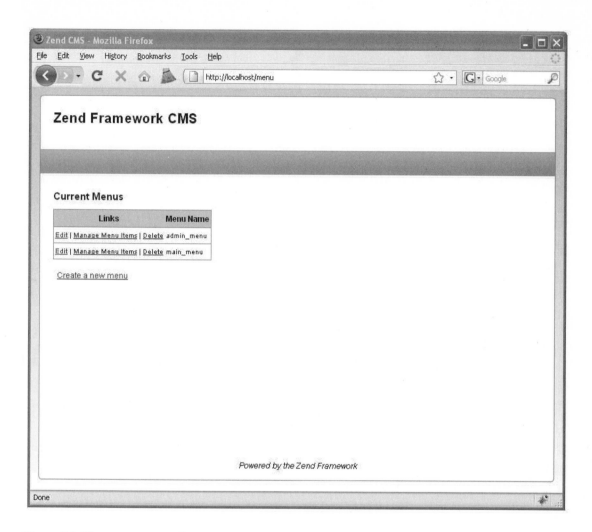

Figure 7-2. The current menu list

Updating a Menu

Now you need to create the updateAction() method in the menu controller. This action will use the existing menu form but will differ from the createAction() method in that it needs to load the menu and populate the form prior to rendering the form.

Opening the Menu to Edit

The first thing you are going to need to do is create an edit action in the menu controller. You can create the edit action method, along with its view script, using Zend_Tool, as shown in Listing 7-18.

Listing 7-18. Creating the Menu Controller Edit Action with Zend_Tool

```
zf create action edit menu
```

Now open the editAction() method in your editor. You are passing this function the ID of the menu to edit as a URL parameter, so you can fetch this using the request object. Next create an instance of the menu form and model. Finally, fetch the menu row, populate the form, and pass it to the view to render, as shown in Listing 7-19.

Listing 7-19. Loading the Menu Form in application/controllers/MenuController.php

```php
public function editAction()
{
    $id = $this->_request->getParam('id');
    $mdlMenu = new Model_Menu();
    $frmMenu = new Form_Menu();
    // fetch the current menu from the db
    $currentMenu = $mdlMenu->find($id)->current();
    // populate the form
    $frmMenu->getElement('id')->setValue($currentMenu->id);
    $frmMenu->getElement('name')->setValue($currentMenu->name);
    $frmMenu->setAction('/menu/edit');
    // pass the form to the view to render
    $this->view->form = $frmMenu;
}
```

Zend_Tool created the edit view script for you in application/views/scripts/menu/edit.phtml. Open this file, add a headline and instructions to it, and then render the form, as shown in Listing 7-20.

Listing 7-20. The Edit Menu View Script in application/views/scripts/menu/edit.phtml

```php
<h2>Update menu</h2>
<p>To update this menu complete this form and click submit...</p>
<?php echo $this->form; ?>
```

Updating the Menu

Now you need to process the form and update the menu. The first thing you need to do is add an updateMenu() method to the menu model. This method will find the menu row and update it (in this case, just update the name and then save it), as shown in Listing 7-21.

Listing 7-21. The updateMenu() Method in application/models/Menu.php

```
public function updateMenu ($id, $name)
{
    $currentMenu = $this->find($id)->current();
    if ($currentMenu) {
        $currentMenu->name = $name;
        return $currentMenu->save();
    } else {
        return false;
    }
}
```

Now you are ready to update the menus. The menu form will post back to the edit action, just as the create action did. You will need to update this action to process the form on the postback. When the form is posted back, you validate the form data and then update the menu if it passes the validation (see Listing 7-22).

Listing 7-22. The Updated editAction() in application/controllers/MenuController.php

```
public function editAction()
{
    $id = $this->_request->getParam('id');
    $mdlMenu = new Model_Menu();
    $frmMenu = new Form_Menu();
    // if this is a postback, then process the form if valid
    if($this->getRequest()->isPost()) {
        if($frmMenu->isValid($_POST)) {
            $menuName = $frmMenu->getValue('name');
            $mdlMenu = new Model_Menu();
            $result = $mdlMenu->updateMenu($id, $menuName);
            if($result) {
                // redirect to the index action
                return $this->_forward('index');
            }
        }
    }else{
        // fetch the current menu from the db
        $currentMenu = $mdlMenu->find($id)->current();
        // populate the form
        $frmMenu->getElement('id')->setValue($currentMenu->id);
        $frmMenu->getElement('name')->setValue($currentMenu->name);
    }
    $frmMenu->setAction('/menu/edit');
    // pass the form to the view to render
    $this->view->form = $frmMenu;
}
```

Deleting Menus

Finally, you need a method to delete an existing menu. This will be very straightforward because it does not require a view, just the deleteAction() in the MenuController and a delete method in the Menu model.

To get started, create the deleteMenu() method in the Menu model. This method will try to find the menu, and if it is successful, it will delete the menu. If not, it will throw an exception (see Listing 7-23).

Listing 7-23. The deleteMenu() Method in application/models/Menu.php

```php
public function deleteMenu($menuId)
{
    $row = $this->find($menuId)->current();
    if($row) {
        return $row->delete();
    }else{
        throw new Zend_Exception("Error loading menu");
    }
}
```

Next create the deleteAction() in the MenuController. To do this with Zend_Tool, use the command in Listing 7-24.

Listing 7-24. Creating the Delete Action in the Menu Controller with Zend_Tool

```
zf create action delete menu
```

Now you need to update the delete action that you just created. You need to fetch the id parameter, create a new instance of the menu model, and run the deleteMenu() method. Once it deletes the menu, it will forward to the admin list in the indexAction(), as shown in Listing 7-25.

Listing 7-25. The deleteAction() in application/controllers/MenuController.php

```php
public function deleteAction()
{
    $id = $this->_request->getParam('id');
    $mdlMenu = new Model_Menu();
    $mdlMenu->deleteMenu($id);
    $this->_forward('index');
}
```

Managing Menu Items

Menus are not much use without menu items. Managing menu items is somewhat more complicated than managing the menus themselves because the site administrator needs more control over them. She needs to be able to define menu labels, create links to menu pages and static links to modules, and control the order in which the menu items are displayed.

Listing the Menu Items

The first thing you are going to want to do is open a menu and create a list of the items in the menu (even though there will not be any yet). If you recall, there was a third link in the admin menu list, which pointed to the index action in the `MenuItemController`. This action will open the menu and then fetch all menu items, passing this information to the view.

To get started, open the menu model and create a method to fetch all the items from a menu named `getItems()`. Note that you could simply use the `Zend_Db_Table_Relationship` instance's `findDependentRowset()` method, but it does not offer the flexibility that you need to sort and conditionally display items. Use the `Zend_Db_Table`'s `select()` object instead so you can programmatically build this query as needed. For now, add a `WHERE` clause to get only the items that are for the menu that was passed, and sort the items by position, as shown in Listing 7-26.

Listing 7-26. The getItemsByMenu() Method in application/models/MenuItem.php

```
public function getItemsByMenu($menuId)
{
    $select = $this->select();
    $select->where("menu_id = ?", $menuId);
    $select->order("position");
    $items = $this->fetchAll($select);
    if($items->count() > 0) {
        return $items;
    }else{
        return null;
    }
}
```

Now that this method is created, you need to update the `indexAction()` to the `MenuItemController`. This action will get the menu that was passed via the URL parameter, create instances of the `Menu` and `MenuItem` models, and then pass the menu details and the menu items to the view, as shown in Listing 7-27.

Listing 7-27. The indexAction() Method in application/controllers/MenuItemController.php

```
public function indexAction()
{
    $menu = $this->_request->getParam('menu');
    $mdlMenu = new Model_Menu();
    $mdlMenuItem = new Model_MenuItem();
    $this->view->menu = $mdlMenu->find($menu)->current();
    $this->view->items = $mdlMenuItem->getItemsByMenu($menu);
}
```

Next update the view script. Open application/views/scripts/menuitem/index.phtml, and set the page title and headline. Then show the user which menu they are working with. Next check and see whether there are any menu items. If there are some, then use the `partialLoop()` helper to render them. If not, display a message letting the user know that there are no items in the menu yet. Finally, add a link to add a new item to the menu. Listing 7-28 shows the complete view script.

Listing 7-28. The Menu Item List in application/views/scripts/menuitem/index.phtml

```
<h2>Manage Menu Items</h2>
<p>Current Menu: <?php echo $this->menu->name;?></p>
<?php
if($this->items != null) {
?>
<table>
    <tr>
        <th>Links </th>
        <th>Label</th>
        <th>Page</th>
        <th>Link</th>
    </tr>
    <?php echo $this->partialLoop('partials/_menu-item-row.phtml',
        $this->items); ?>
</table>
<?php }else{?>
<p>This menu does not have any items yet.</p>
<?php }?>
    <p><a href='/menuitem/add/menu/<?php echo $this->menu->id ?>'>Add a new item</a></p>
```

Now create the partial script to render the menu item row. This will be very similar to the partial script you created for the menus, with one exception; you need to add links to move the menu item up or down in the list.

Add a new file named _menu-item-row.phtml to the partials folder. Since only some of the menu items link to pages, you need to first check what kind of item it is. If it is a page link, then you need to load the page so you can display the title rather than the ID that the CMS uses to reference the item. Then render the table row. Create links to update the item, move it up or down, and delete it. Then render the item label, the page title (if it exists), and the link (see Listing 7-29).

Listing 7-29. The Menu Item List in application/views/scripts/partials/_menu-item-row.phtml

```
<?php
    if($this->page_id > 0) {
        $page = new CMS_Content_Item_Page($this->page_id);
        $pageName = $page->name;
    }else{
        $pageName = null;
    }
?>
<tr>
    <td class='links'>
        <a href='/menuitem/update/id/<?php echo $this->id;?>'>Update</a> |
        <a href='/menuitem/move/direction/up/id/<?php echo $this->id;?>'>
            Move up</a> |
        <a href='/menuitem/move/direction/down/id/<?php echo $this->id;?>'>
            Move down</a> |
        <a href='/menuitem/delete/id/<?php echo $this->id;?>'>Delete</a>
    </td>
    <td><?php echo $this->label ?></td>
    <td><?php echo $pageName ?></td>
```

```
    <td><?php echo $this->link ?></td>
</tr>
```

Adding New Menu Items

Now you need to create the method to create new menu items. This will be similar to the rest of the create actions, with the exception that you need to keep track of the parent menu ID.

The Menu Item Form

The menu item form requires two hidden fields, one for the item ID and one for the parent menu ID. It also requires a text field for the label, a select control for the page, and another text field for the link (which will be used if the page is not set). The only thing that is different with this form is that you need to load all the current pages as options for the select page control. Listing 7-30 shows the completed form.

Listing 7-30. The Menu Item Form in application/forms/MenuItem.php

```php
<?php
class Form_MenuItem extends Zend_Form
{
    public function init()
    {
        $this->setMethod('post');

        // create new element
        $id = $this->createElement('hidden', 'id');
        // element options
        $id->setDecorators(array('ViewHelper'));
        // add the element to the form
        $this->addElement($id);

        // create new element
        $menuId = $this->createElement('hidden', 'menu_id');
        // element options
        $menuId->setDecorators(array('ViewHelper'));
        // add the element to the form
        $this->addElement($menuId);

        // create new element
        $label = $this->createElement('text', 'label');
        // element options
        $label->setLabel('Label: ');
        $label->setRequired(TRUE);
        $label->addFilter('StripTags');
        $label->setAttrib('size',40);
        // add the element to the form
        $this->addElement($label);
```

```
    // create new element
    $pageId = $this->createElement('select', 'page_id');
    // element options
    $pageId->setLabel('Select a page to link to: ');
    $pageId->setRequired(true);

    // populate this with the pages
    $mdlPage = new Model_Page();
    $pages = $mdlPage->fetchAll(null, 'name');
    $pageId->addMultiOption(0, 'None');
    if($pages->count() > 0) {
        foreach ($pages as $page) {
            $pageId->addMultiOption($page->id, $page->name);
        }
    }
    // add the element to the form
    $this->addElement($pageId);

    // create new element
    $link = $this->createElement('text', 'link');
    // element options
    $link->setLabel('or specify a link: ');
    $link->setRequired(false);
    $link->setAttrib('size',50);
    // add the element to the form
    $this->addElement($link);

    $submit = $this->addElement('submit', 'submit', array('label' => 'Submit'));
    }
}
?>
```

Creating the Add Menu Item Action

Now add the addAction() method to the MenuitemController. You can do this with Zend_Tool, as demonstrated in Listing 7-31, or simply add this code manually.

Listing 7-31. Creating the menuitem Controller Add Action using Zend_Tool

```
zf create action add menuitem
```

The add action should load the menu that was passed via the id URL parameter, load the form, and populate the form with the menu ID. Then pass the form to the view to render it, as shown in Listing 7-32.

Listing 7-32. The addAction() in application/controllers/MenuItemController.php

```
public function addAction()
{
```

```
$menu = $this->_request->getParam('menu');
$mdlMenu = new Model_Menu();
$this->view->menu = $mdlMenu->find($menu)->current();
$frmMenuItem = new Form_MenuItem();
$frmMenuItem->populate(array('menu_id' => $menu));
$this->view->form = $frmMenuItem;
}
```

Rendering the Menu Item Form

Next you need to update the add menu item form. Open the
application/views/scripts/menuitem/add.phtml file that Zend_Tool created, and set the page headline.
Then display the current menu so the user can keep track of what they are working on and render the
form, as shown in Listing 7-33.

Listing 7-33. Rendering the cadd menu item form in application/views/scripts/menu-item/add.phtml

```
<h2>Add Menu Item</h2>
<p>Current Menu: <?php echo $this->menu->name;?></p>
<p>To add a menu item fill out the form below and click submit...</p>
<?php echo $this->form; ?>
```

Processing the Form

Now you need to process the create menu item form. Create a new method in the MenuItem model to add
the menu item. This method will work much like the other add/create methods with two exceptions.
First, it needs to enter the parent menu ID, and second, it needs to set the item's position (Listing 7-34).
You will set up the methods to manage the menu position in one moment.

Listing 7-34. The addItem() Method in application/models/MenuItem.php

```
public function addItem($menuId, $label, $pageId = 0, $link = null)
{
    $row = $this->createRow();
    $row->menu_id = $menuId;
    $row->label = $label;
    $row->page_id = $pageId;
    $row->link = $link;
    // note that you wil create the _getLastPosition method in listing 7-36
    $row->position = $this->_getLastPosition($menuId) + 1;
    return $row->save();
}
```

Next update the addAction() method in the MenuItemController to process the form on the
postback, as shown in Listing 7-35. It needs to go through the standard process of checking to see
whether the form has been posted back and then validating the form data and creating the item if the
data is OK. It then forwards back to the menu item list.

Listing 7-35. The Updated addAction() in application/controllers/MenuitemController.php

```
public function addAction ()
{
    $menu = $this->_request->getParam('menu');
    $mdlMenu = new Model_Menu();
    $this->view->menu = $mdlMenu->find($menu)->current();
    $frmMenuItem = new Form_MenuItem();
    if ($this->_request->isPost()) {
        if ($frmMenuItem->isValid($_POST)) {
            $data = $frmMenuItem->getValues();
            $mdlMenuItem = new Model_MenuItem();
            $mdlMenuItem->addItem($data['menu_id'], $data['label'],
                $data['page_id'], $data['link']);
            $this->_request->setParam('menu', $data['menu_id']);
            $this->_forward('index');
        }
    }
    $frmMenuItem->populate(array('menu_id' => $menu));
    $this->view->form = $frmMenuItem;
}
```

Sorting Menu Items

One challenge with managing menus is sorting them. The MVC approach does make this somewhat cleaner by separating the sorting logic from the application's functionality.

To start with, create the methods that will perform the sorting in the MenuItem model. This will require three methods:

- _getLastPosition(): This method will get the last (highest) position in the selected menu and is a utility method that the MenuItem model uses (as in the addItem() method).

- moveUp(): This method moves the selected menu item up.

- moveDown(): This method moves the selected menu item down.

The first method you will create is the _getLastPosition() method, because the other methods will require it to function. This method is a straightforward function that uses the Zend_Db_Table's select() object to sort the items by position (descending) and filter them by the parent menu ID. It then uses the fetchRow() method to fetch a single row, which is the highest. If there are no results, then it returns 0. Listing 7-36 shows the complete method.

Listing 7-36. The_getLastPosition() Method in application/models/MenuItem.php

```
    private function _getLastPosition ($menuId)
    {
        $select = $this->select();
        $select->where("menu_id = ?", $menuId);
        $select->order('position DESC');
        $row = $this->fetchRow($select);
```

```
        if ($row) {
            return $row->position;
        } else {
            return 0;
        }
    }
```

Next you need to create the methods to move the menu item up and down. Start with the moveUp() method. This method needs to load the menu item. If it does not find the menu item, then throw an exception. Next you need to check the current menu position. If it is already the first item, return false. Otherwise, find the previous item in the menu. Once you find this row, switch the positions, and save both rows (Listing 7-37).

Listing 7-37. The moveUp() Method in application/models/MenuItem.php

```
public function moveUp($itemId)
{
    $row = $this->find($itemId)->current();
    if($row) {
        $position = $row->position;
        if($position < 1) {
                // this is already the first item
                return FALSE;
        }else{
            //find the previous item
            $select = $this->select();
         $select->order('position DESC');
            $select->where("position < ?", $position);
            $select->where("menu_id = ?", $row->menu_id);
            $previousItem = $this->fetchRow($select);
            if($previousItem) {
                //switch positions with the previous item
                $previousPosition = $previousItem->position;
                $previousItem->position = $position;
                $previousItem->save();
                $row->position = $previousPosition;
                $row->save();
            }
        }
    } else {
        throw new Zend_Exception("Error loading menu item");
    }
}
```

Next do the moveDown() method. This method will also fetch the current item, as with the moveUp() method. Then it checks to see whether the item is already the last item and returns false if it is. If not, it finds the next item and switches positions with it. Listing 7-38 shows the complete moveDown() method.

Listing 7-38. The moveDown() Method in application/models/MenuItem.php

```
public function moveDown($itemId) {
    $row = $this->find ( $itemId )->current ();
    if ($row) {
        $position = $row->position;
        if ($position == $this->_getLastPosition ( $row->menu_id )) {
            // this is already the last item
            return FALSE;
        } else {
            //find the next item
            $select = $this->select ();
            $select->order ( 'position ASC' );
            $select->where ( "position > ?", $position );
                    $select->where("menu_id = ?", $row->menu_id);
            $nextItem = $this->fetchRow ( $select );
            if ($nextItem) {
                //switch positions with the next item
                $nextPosition = $nextItem->position;
                $nextItem->position = $position;
                $nextItem->save ();
                $row->position = $nextPosition;
                $row->save ();
            }
        }
    } else {
        throw new Zend_Exception ( "Error loading menu item" );
    }
}
```

Now that you have the model methods to manage the menu item positions, you can create the
moveAction() method in the MenuItemModel (Listing 7-39). This action will be relatively simple because it
does not require a view or a form. It requires two URL parameters: the ID of the menu item and the
direction to move it. Once it fetches these values, it loads the requested menu item, and then it runs
either moveUp() or moveDown(), depending on the value of the direction parameter. Finally, it sets the
menu parameter (since the index action expects this) and redirects to the indexAction().

Note Some controller actions just perform an action and then forward to another action to render. In these
cases, I often just write the method rather than using Zend_Tool. Zend_Tool will always create the view script,
even for forwarding actions.

Listing 7-39. The moveAction() in application/controllers/MenuItemController.php

```
public function moveAction() {
    $id = $this->_request->getParam ( 'id' );
    $direction = $this->_request->getParam ( 'direction' );
```

```
$mdlMenuItem = new Model_MenuItem ( );
$menuItem = $mdlMenuItem->find ( $id )->current ();
if ($direction == 'up') {
    $mdlMenuItem->moveUp ( $id );
} elseif ($direction == 'down') {
    $mdlMenuItem->moveDown ( $id );
}
$this->_request->setParam ( 'menu', $menuItem->menu_id );
$this->_forward ( 'index' );
}
```

Updating Menu Items

The next step is updating the menu items. This will function exactly the same as the updateAction() method in the MenuController.

Loading the Update Item Form

Create the menu item update action using Zend_Tool, as shown in Listing 7-40.

Listing 7-40. Creating the Update Menu Item Action Using Zend_Tool

```
zf create action update menuitem
```

Then fill in the update action. The menu item ID will be passed to this action as a URL parameter, so get this value. Then load the menu item and its parent menu. Fetch a new instance of the menu item form. Then populate the form with the menu item row, and pass the form to the view. See Listing 7-41 for the completed action.

Listing 7-41. Loading the Menu Form in the updateAction() of the MenuItemController in application/controllers/MenuItemController.php

```
public function updateAction()
{
    $id = $this->_request->getParam ( 'id' );
    // fetch the current item
    $mdlMenuItem = new Model_MenuItem ( );
    $currentMenuItem = $mdlMenuItem->find ( $id )->current ();
    // fetch its menu
    $mdlMenu = new Model_Menu ( );
    $this->view->menu = $mdlMenu->find ( $currentMenuItem->menu_id )->current ();
    // create and populate the form instance
    $frmMenuItem = new Form_MenuItem();
        $frmMenuItem->setAction('/menuitem/update');
    $frmMenuItem->populate ( $currentMenuItem->toArray () );
    $this->view->form = $frmMenuItem;
}
```

Rendering the Update Item Form

Now you need to render the update form. Zend_Tool created a view script for the update action in application/views/scripts/menuitem/update.phtml. Open this file in your editor. Render a headline and the current menu name on this page, and then render the form, as shown in Listing 7-42.

Listing 7-42. Rendering the Update Page Form in application/views/scripts/menuitem/update.phtml

```
<h2>Update Menu Item</h2>
<p>Current Menu: <?php echo $this->menu->name;?></p>
<p>To update this menu item fill out the form below and click submit...</p>
<?php echo $this->form; ?>
```

Processing the Update Item Form

The next step is processing the update form when it is posted back. First, create a new function to update the menu item in the MenuItem model. This method should find the row it needs to update. If it doesn't find the row, then throw a new Zend_Exception. Next update the page label and the page_id. Then you need to check the value of the page_id; if it is less than 1 (not set), then you should use the value of the link, which is what will be used for static links to modules. Note that the menu_id is not one of the parameters in this method; you can't change the menu an item is in. Listing 7-43 shows the completed updateItem() method.

Listing 7-43. The updateItem() in application/models/MenuItem.php

```
public function updateItem($itemId, $label, $pageId = 0, $link = null) {
    $row = $this->find ( $itemId )->current ();
    if ($row) {
        $row->label = $label;
        $row->page_id = $pageId;
        if ($pageId < 1) {
            $row->link = $link;
        } else {
            $row->link = null;
        }
        return $row->save ();
    } else {
        throw new Zend_Exception ( "Error loading menu item" );
    }
}
```

Now you can update the updateAction() in the MenuItemController to process the form. This will process the form much like the updateAction() did in the MenuController, with one difference. Since you manage menu items based on the menu, then you need to set the menu parameter before forwarding to the indexAction(). See Listing 7-44 for the completed action.

Listing 7-44. The Updated updateAction() in application/controllers/MenuitemController.php

```php
public function updateAction ()
{
    $id = $this->_request->getParam('id');
    // fetch the current item
    $mdlMenuItem = new Model_MenuItem();
    $currentMenuItem = $mdlMenuItem->find($id)->current();
    // fetch its menu
    $mdlMenu = new Model_Menu();
    $this->view->menu = $mdlMenu->find($currentMenuItem->menu_id)->current();
    // create and populate the form instance
    $frmMenuItem = new Form_MenuItem();
    $frmMenuItem->setAction('/menuitem/update');
    // process the postback
    if ($this->_request->isPost()) {
        if ($frmMenuItem->isValid($_POST)) {
            $data = $frmMenuItem->getValues();
            $mdlMenuItem->updateItem($data['id'], $data['label'],
                $data['page_id'], $data['link']);
            $this->_request->setParam('menu', $data['menu_id']);
            return $this->_forward('index');
        }
    } else {
        $frmMenuItem->populate($currentMenuItem->toArray());
    }
    $this->view->form = $frmMenuItem;
}
```

Deleting Menu Items

The final step in managing menus is deleting menu items. This will be very straightforward because it does not require a view, just the deleteAction() method in the MenuItemController and a deleteItem() method in the MenuItem model.

To get started, create the deleteItem() method in the MenuItem model. This method will try to find the menu, and if it is successful, it will delete the menu. If not, it will throw an exception, as shown in Listing 7-45.

Listing 7-45. The deleteItem() Method in application/models/MenuItem.php

```php
public function deleteItem($itemId) {
    $row = $this->find ( $itemId )->current ();
    if ($row) {
        return $row->delete ();
    } else {
        throw new Zend_Exception ( "Error loading menu item" );
    }
}
```

Next create the deleteAction() method in the MenuItemController. This action will create a new instance of the MenuItem model and find the menu item that matches the ID that was passed to the action in the URL parameter. Next it runs the deleteItem() method. Then it sets the menu parameter and forwards to the indexAction() method. Listing 7-46 shows the complete method.

Listing 7-46. The deleteAction() Method in application/controllers/MenuItemController.php

```
public function deleteAction() {
    $id = $this->_request->getParam ( 'id' );
    $mdlMenuItem = new Model_MenuItem ( );
    $currentMenuItem = $mdlMenuItem->find ( $id )->current ();
    $mdlMenuItem->deleteItem ( $id );
    $this->_request->setParam ( 'menu', $currentMenuItem->menu_id );
    $this->_forward ( 'index' );
}
```

Rendering Menus

Now that the menu management component is complete, you are ready to render the menus. To do this, create a new action in the MenuController named renderAction(). You can do this with Zend_Tool, as shown in Listing 7-47.

Listing 7-47. Creating the Render Menu Action with Zend_Tool

```
zf create action render menu
```

Zend_Navigation is a new component that has been developed to make managing your site navigation as easy as possible. To use Zend_Navigation, you need to first fetch all items from the requested menu. Then load each of those items into an array. When this is complete, you create a new instance of Zend_Navigation, which you pass the array to. Finally, you pass this to the Zend_View navigation helper, as shown in Listing 7-48.

Listing 7-48. The renderAction() Method in application/controllers/MenuController.php

```
public function renderAction()
{
    $menu = $this->_request->getParam ( 'menu' );
    $mdlMenuItems = new Model_MenuItem ( );
    $menuItems = $mdlMenuItems->getItemsByMenu ( $menu );

    if(count($menuItems) > 0) {
        foreach ($menuItems as $item) {
            $label = $item->label;
            if(!empty($item->link)) {
                $uri = $item->link;
            }else{
                $uri = '/page/open/id/' . $item->page_id;
            }
```

```
            $itemArray[] = array(
                'label'        => $label,
                'uri'          => $uri
            );
        }
        $container = new Zend_Navigation($itemArray);
        $this->view->navigation()->setContainer($container);
    }
}
```

Now you need to update the view script that Zend_Tool created. Since you have already loaded the navigation helper, it is ready to render. You call its menu() method to render it as a menu, as shown in Listing 7-49.

Listing 7-49. The Render Menu View Script in application/views/scripts/menu/render.phtml

```
<?php echo $this->navigation()->menu(); ?>
```

Creating the Main Site Menus

With the menu management component complete, you can create the main site menus. For right now, create two menus: the main menu and the admin menu.

Creating the Main Menus

To create the main menu, point your browser to http://localhost/menu/create, and create a new menu named main_menu. Then click the Manage Menu Items link on the menu list, and add a few items (whatever you want) to this menu. To make managing the CMS easier, you will probably want to create an admin menu. Point your browser to /menu/create, and create a new menu named admin_menu. Then click the Manage Menu Items link on the menu list. Add each of the menu items in Table 7-1.

Table 7-1. The Admin Menu Items

Label	Link
Manage Content	/page
Manage Menus	/menu

Setting the Main Menu GUIDs

You generally do not want to hard-code a GUID into your scripts if you can avoid it, since this is something that can be changed through the CMS. Instead, it is preferable to set the GUIDs for these items in a config file or in the application bootstrap. In this case, use the latter, as you did with the view skin. Create a new method in the Bootstrap.php file named _initMenus(). Fetch the view from the bootstrap and then pass the menu ids to the view, as shown in Listing 7-50.

Listing 7-50. The initMenus() Method in application/Bootstrap.php

```
protected function _initMenus ()
{
    $view = $this->getResource('view');
    $view->mainMenuId = 1;
    $view->adminMenuId = 2;
}
```

Rendering the Main Menus

There are already placeholders for the main menu and admin menu in the site layout file. Open application/layouts/scripts/layout.phtml. Now render the main menu using the Zend_View action() helper. The action() helper enables you to call a different controller action from the view; the helper then returns the response that the action renders. Behind the scenes it clones the request so you should always consider this overhead when you use it. I prefer to set these placeholders at the top of the page. This makes it possible to fetch information from them throughout the page (Listing 7-51).

Listing 7-51. Rendering the Main Menu in application/layouts/scripts/layout.phtml

```
$this->layout()->nav = $this->action('render', 'menu', null,
    array('menu' => $this->mainMenuId));
```

Now you should update the styles for the #nav div to make your menu look more like a menu and less like a list. First create a new CSS file in your blues skin named nav.css. Then add this file to the skin.xml file in the root of the blues skin. Locate the <stylesheet> section, and add the reference to nav.css, as shown in Listing 7-52.

Listing 7-52. The nav.css Reference to Add into public/skins/blues/skin.xml

```
<stylesheet>nav.css</stylesheet>
```

Next style this menu. Add the CSS from Listing 7-53 into the new nav.css file.

Listing 7-53. The Nav Style in public/skins/blues/css/nav.css

```
@CHARSET "ISO-8859-1";
#nav ul{
    list-style:none;
}

#nav ul li{
    display:inline;
    padding:0 20px;
}

#nav ul li a{
    font-family:"Arial Black";
```

```
    color:#FCE6C8;
    font-size:16px;
    text-decoration:none;
}

#nav ul li a:hover{
    color:#fff;
}

#nav ul li a.selected{
    font-weight:bold;
}
```

Rendering the Admin Menu

In the next chapter, you are going to learn about Zend Framework security. You will update this menu to render conditionally depending on the current user's permission. For now, you can just render the menu in the placeholder (Listing 7-54).

Listing 7-54. Rendering the Main Menu in application/layouts/scripts/layout.phtml

```
$this->layout()->adminMenu = $this->action(
    'render', 'menu', null, array('menu' => $this->adminMenuId)
);
```

Now when you point your browser at http://localhost, you should see both of your menus rendering, as shown in Figure 7-3.

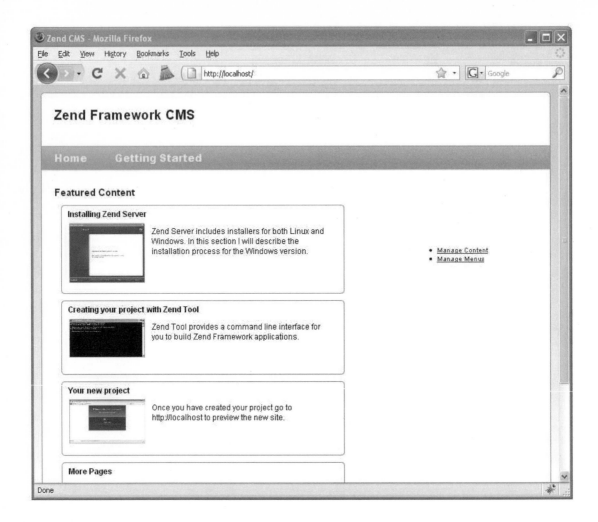

Figure 7-3. The home page with menus

Creating SEO-Friendly URLs

One final note on navigation is search engine optimization (SEO). Most people are very sensitive about SEO-friendly URLs now, as well they should be. It looks better if nothing else. Zend Framework follows the best practices by default, since it does not rely on long query strings. The way the CMS is set up also makes it fairly easy to introduce simple SEO-friendly URLs after the fact. Keep in mind that it is possible to make these much more attractive, but for now just set the CMS up to use the page title rather than the ID. You will need to update two files to do this: the `PageController` and the `MenuController`.

Note If you do turn on SEO friendly URLs, you should add an index to the pages table on the title column.

Start by updating the MenuController's render action (Listing 7-55).

Listing 7-55. The Updated renderAction() Method in application/controllers/MenuController.php

```
public function renderAction()
{
    $menu = $this->_request->getParam ( 'menu' );
    $mdlMenuItems = new Model_MenuItem ( );
    $menuItems = $mdlMenuItems->getItemsByMenu ( $menu );

    if(count($menuItems) > 0) {
        foreach ($menuItems as $item) {
            $label = $item->label;
            if(!empty($item->link)) {
                $uri = $item->link;
            }else{
                // update this to form more search-engine-friendly URLs
                $page = new CMS_Content_Item_Page($item->page_id);
                $uri = '/page/open/title/' . $page->name;
            }
            $itemArray[] = array(
                'label'         => $label,
                'uri'           => $uri
            );
        }
        $container = new Zend_Navigation($itemArray);
        $this->view->navigation()->setContainer($container);
    }
}
```

Now that the menu is using the title in the URL, you need to update the page controller's openAction() to fetch the page by the title rather than ID, as shown in Listing 7-56.

Listing 7-56. The Updated openAction() in application/controllers/PageController.php

```
public function openAction()
{
    $title = $this->_request->getParam('title');
    $id = $this->_request->getParam('id');
    // first confirm the page exists
    $mdlPage = new Model_Page();
    $select = $mdlPage->select();
    $select->where('name = ?', $title);
    $row = $mdlPage->fetchRow($select);
    if($row) {
```

```
        $this->view->page = new CMS_Content_Item_Page($row->id);
    }else{
        // the error handler will catch this exception
        throw new Zend_Controller_Action_Exception(
            "The page you requested was not found", 404);
    }
}
```

Summary

In this chapter, you added navigation management to your CMS project.

You started by creating new menus, which involved creating a form, a model, and a controller for them. Then you updated and deleted the menus. In the next part, you worked with menu items. The menu items' CRUD functionality was virtually identical to that of the menus.

Once this was done, you created a method to load the menu items into the Zend_Navigation component and render them. You then used these tools to create the actual site and admin menus, which you added to the site layout file.

Finally, you updated the menus to use more neatly formed, SEO-friendly URLs.

CHAPTER 8

Handling Security in a Zend Framework Project

Security should be the first and foremost concern of any web application project. The same tools that you are building to make it easy for your clients to manage their sites can be leveraged by hackers if you're not careful. This is a serious responsibility that should not be taken lightly.

The good news is that the Zend Framework developers take security very seriously and have built a stable, well-tested set of components that make it easier to write more secure programs. These components include Zend_Auth and Zend_Acl.

- Zend_Auth is solely concerned with authenticating (and persisting) the application users.

- Zend_Acl handles resources (pages), roles (user roles), and which roles can access which resources.

By separating these areas of responsibility, you are able to manage users, and the access they are allowed, depending on the unique needs of your particular project.

In the case of the CMS you're building in this book, you will manage the users with the database; you already have the database set up for the content, so this will be the easiest way. Implementing your site security scheme encompasses several steps:

1. Create the tools to manage users.

2. Create a way for users to log in and out.

3. Add access control to security-sensitive parts of the site.

4. Integrate the access control into the application.

Managing CMS Users

Anyone who visits a site can be considered a user. From an anonymous visitor to your site administrators, everyone has a role. The CMS uses these roles to determine whether the user has permission to access restricted areas of the site or specific resources, such as files. You can have as many roles as you need, but I generally try to keep things as simple as possible. Initially, you will have two roles:

- *Users*: These are registered users who don't have admin privileges.

- *Administrators*: These are the site managers who can access any area of the CMS.

User Data and Model

As mentioned earlier, you will store the CMS user data in a database table. At a minimum, this table will need to store the username, password, and role. You will also add fields for a user's first and last names. You can add or remove fields depending on your specific project. To create the users table, run the SQL statement shown in Listing 8-1.

Listing 8-1. SQL Statement to Create the users Table

```
CREATE TABLE `users` (
  `id` int(11) NOT NULL auto_increment,
  `username` varchar(50) default NULL,
  `password` varchar(250) default NULL,
  `first_name` varchar(50) default NULL,
  `last_name` varchar(50) default NULL,
  `role` varchar(25) default NULL,
  PRIMARY KEY  (`id`)
) DEFAULT CHARSET=utf8;
```

Now that you've created the users table, you need to set up a model to manage it. Create a file in the application/models folder named User.php. Open this file, and create the User model class, as shown in Listing 8-2.

Listing 8-2. The User Model Class in application/user/models/User.php

```
<?php
require_once 'Zend/Db/Table/Abstract.php';
class Model_User extends Zend_Db_Table_Abstract {
    /**
     * The default table name
     */
    protected $_name = 'users';
}
```

Creating a New User

The process of managing your users will be very similar to that of your pages and menus. This consistency makes it much easier to both develop and maintain applications.

Creating the User Controller

Now that you have the user model set up, the next step is to create a controller to manage the users. You can do this with Zend_Tool using the command in Listing 8-3.

Listing 8-3. Creating the User Controller with Zend_Tool

```
zf create controller user
```

This will create the controller, its view folder, and the index action/view script.

Creating the User Form

Now you're ready to create the user form. Create a new file in application/forms named User.php, and then create the new user form, as shown in Listing 8-4.

Listing 8-4. The User Form in application/forms/User.php

```php
<?php
class Form_User extends Zend_Form
{
    public function init()
    {
        $this->setMethod('post');

        // create new element
        $id = $this->createElement('hidden', 'id');
        // element options
        $id->setDecorators(array('ViewHelper'));
        // add the element to the form
        $this->addElement($id);

        //create the form elements
        $username = $this->createElement('text','username');
        $username->setLabel('Username: ');
        $username->setRequired('true');
        $username->addFilter('StripTags');
        $username->addErrorMessage('The username is required!');
        $this->addElement($username);

        $password = $this->createElement('password', 'password');
        $password->setLabel('Password: ');
        $password->setRequired('true');
        $this->addElement($password);

        $firstName = $this->createElement('text','first_name');
        $firstName->setLabel('First Name: ');
        $firstName->setRequired('true');
        $firstName->addFilter('StripTags');
        $this->addElement($firstName);

        $lastName = $this->createElement('text','last_name');
        $lastName->setLabel('Last Name: ');
        $lastName->setRequired('true');
        $lastName->addFilter('StripTags');
        $this->addElement($lastName);

        $role = $this->createElement('select', 'role');
```

```
        $role->setLabel("Select a role:");
        $role->addMultiOption('User', 'user');
        $role->addMultiOption('Administrator', 'administrator');
        $this->addElement($role);

        $submit = $this->addElement('submit', 'submit', array('label' => 'Submit'));
    }
}
?>
```

Rendering the Create User Form

Once the form is set up, the next step is to render it. This requires a controller action and view script. You can create this action and view script with Zend_Tool using the command in Listing 8-5.

Listing 8-5. Creating the create user Action with Zend_Tool

```
zf create action create user
```

This command creates the createAction() method in the user controller. Open the user controller, and locate this method. Now create a new instance of the user form, and set the form action to /user/create, as shown in Listing 8-6. Then pass the form instance to the view to render.

Listing 8-6. Loading the Create User Form in application/controllers/UserController.php

```
public function createAction()
{
    $userForm = new Form_User();
    $userForm->setAction('/user/create');
    $this->view->form = $userForm;
}
```

The next step is to update the view script that Zend_Tool created. Open application/views/scripts/user/create.phtml, and set the page title and headline as you did with the view scripts you created earlier. Then render the form. You can do this by simply echoing it; Zend_Form has a view helper that builds the form's XHTML and renders it, as shown in Listing 8-7.

Listing 8-7. The Create User View in application/user/views/scripts/user/create.phtml

```
<h2>Create a new user</h2>
<p>To create a new admin user complete this form and click submit...</p>
<?php echo $this->form; ?>
```

Now if you point your browser to http://localhost/user/create, you should see the create user form, as shown in Figure 8-1.

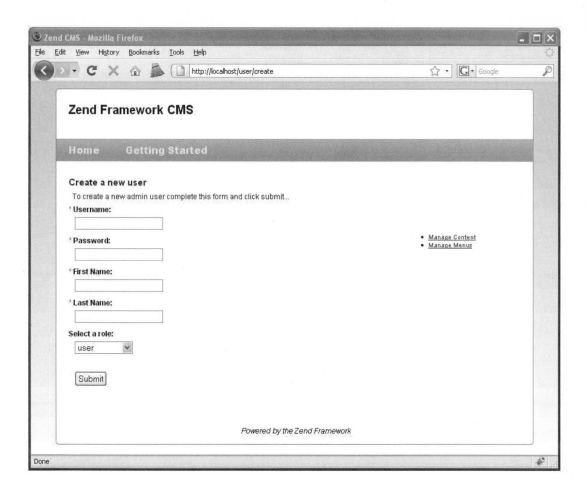

Figure 8-1. The create user form

Processing the Form

Processing the form is a two-step process. The controller will load and validate the data but will rely on the User model to write the data to the database.

You can use the Zend_Db_Table method directly from the controller, but I prefer to add a method to the model class to do this. You will create this function first and then update the controller. Open the User model class, and add a createUser method. This method will need to take the username, password, first name, last name, and admin role as arguments. It will first create a new row and then set each of the column values (Listing 8-8).

Listing 8-8. The createUser Method in application/user/models/User.php

```php
public function createUser($username, $password, $firstName, $lastName, $role)
{
    // create a new row
    $rowUser = $this->createRow();
    if($rowUser) {
        // update the row values
        $rowUser->username = $username;
        $rowUser->password = md5($password);
        $rowUser->first_name = $firstName;
        $rowUser->last_name = $lastName;
        $rowUser->role = $role;
        $rowUser->save();
        //return the new user
        return $rowUser;
    } else {
        throw new Zend_Exception("Could not create user!");
    }
}
```

Now that you have the method to add a new user to the database, you are ready to process the form. When you submit the create user form, it posts back to the createAction() method in the user controller, but the action does nothing but load and render the form. You need to update this function so it detects whether the form has been posted back. You do this with the request->isPost() function. If it is posted back, then populate the form with the POST data, and check to see whether the form is valid. If it is, you pass the form data to the createUser method and redirect to the list action, which you will create in the next section (see Listing 8-9).

Listing 8-9. The Updated createAction in application/user/controllers/UserController.php

```php
public function createAction ()
{
    $userForm = new Form_User();
    if ($this->_request->isPost()) {
        if ($userForm->isValid($_POST)) {
            $userModel = new Model_User();
            $userModel->createUser(
                $userForm->getValue('username'),
                $userForm->getValue('password'),
                $userForm->getValue('first_name'),
                $userForm->getValue('last_name'),
                $userForm->getValue('role')
            );
            return $this->_forward('list');        }
    }
    $userForm->setAction('/user/create');
    $this->view->form = $userForm;
}
```

Managing Existing Users

Now that there is a way to add users to the database, you need a way to manage them. First you will need a list of all the current users. The best way to do this is to create a new method in the user model. I like to use static methods for these types of functions; it makes the method easier to use. Create a new static method in the user model to get the current users, as in Listing 8-10.

Listing 8-10. Getting the Users from application/user/models/User.php

```php
public static function getUsers()
{
    $userModel = new self();
    $select = $userModel->select();
    $select->order(array('last_name', 'first_name'));
    return $userModel->fetchAll($select);
}
```

Then you need methods to update their accounts and delete them if necessary. To get started, create the list user action with Zend_Tool using the command in Listing 8-11.

Listing 8-11. Creating the list user Action with Zend_Tool

```
zf create action list user
```

Since there will be no form processing done in the listAction() method, it is very simple. It will just load the current users and pass them to the view.

First create an instance of the user model. Then fetch all the current users. If the query returns users, then pass them to the view to render, as shown in Listing 8-12.

Listing 8-12. The list users Action in application/controllers/UserController.php

```php
public function listAction ()
{
    $currentUsers = Model_User::getUsers();
    if ($currentUsers->count() > 0) {
        $this->view->users = $currentUsers;
    } else {
        $this->view->users = null;
    }
}
```

The index view script will be a little more complicated than the previous ones. It needs to display a list of all the current users. Zend_View makes this very easy with its partialLoop() helper. This helper takes two arguments: the path to a script to render for each row and the data. You will render the users in a table, so this partialLoop will need to render a table row for each user. You will need to create this partial script first. Create a new file in application/views/scripts/partials named _user-row.phtml.

This partial script will render a table row. It needs fields for the user's username, first name, last name, and role. It also needs to render links to update and delete the user. Note that the partialLoop helper casts the values of the row to view variables, as shown in Listing 8-13.

151

Listing 8-13. User Row Partial in application/views/scripts/partials/_user-row.phtml

```
<tr>
    <td class='links'>
        <a href='/user/update/id/<?php echo $this->id;?>'>Update</a>
        <a href='/user/delete/id/<?php echo $this->id;?>'>Delete</a>
    </td>
    <td><?php echo $this->last_name ?></td>
    <td><?php echo $this->first_name ?></td>
    <td><?php echo $this->username ?></td>
    <td><?php echo $this->role ?></td>
</tr>
```

With the data and partial in place, you are ready to create the index view script. First you need to set the page title and headline. Then check whether there are any users. If there are, then create a table and let the partialLoop helper render the user rows. If there are no users, then display a message. You should also add a create user link since it will be the main user management page (Listing 8-14).

Listing 8-14. The User List in application/views/scripts/user/list.phtml

```
<h2>Current Users</h2>
<?php
if($this->users != null) {
?>
<table class='spreadsheet' cellpadding='0' cellspacing='0'>
    <tr>
        <th>Links</th>
        <th>Last Name</th>
        <th>First Name</th>
        <th>Username</th>
        <th>Role</th>
        <th>
    </tr>
    <?php echo $this->partialLoop('partials/_user-row.phtml', $this->users); ?>
</table>
<?php }else{?>
<p>You do not have any users yet.</p>
<?php }?>
<p><a href='/user/create'>Create a new user</a></p>
```

Once this is done, add a few test users. After you successfully create a new user, you should be directed to the list page, which looks like Figure 8-2.

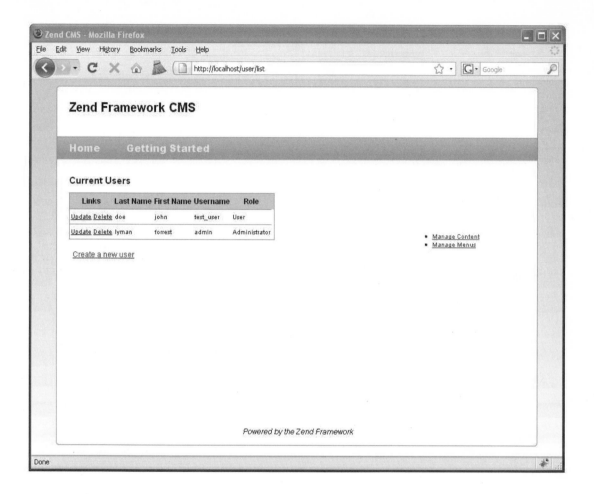

Figure 8-2. The user list

You should note that the user row has links to update or delete the user. These links assume that there is an update and a delete action in the user controller, which you will create next.

Note The user list view will be the main admin page for CMS users. You may want to add this page to the admin menu that you created in Chapter 7.

Updating Users

Updating a user is similar to creating a user in many ways. If a form has been posted back, it processes it. If not, it renders the form, loading it with the user's current account information.

The first thing you need to do is create the update user action. You can do this with Zend_Tool, as shown in Listing 8-15.

Listing 8-15. Creating the update user Action with Zend_Tool

```
zf create action update user
```

Now open the updateAction() method in the user controller. In this method, you need to create a new instance of the user form.

Now you need to remove the password element from the form. This is done because the password is encrypted using one-way encryption, which means that you can't just fetch the value to populate the password field.

The user list passed the user's ID as a URL parameter; you need to fetch it and load the user row. Then you need to load the user form with this data and pass it to the view to render, as shown in Listing 8-16.

Listing 8-16. The update user Action in application/controllers/UserController.php

```php
public function updateAction ()
{
    $userForm = new Form_User();
    $userForm->setAction('/user/update');
    $userForm->removeElement('password');
    $id = $this->_request->getParam('id');
    $userModel = new Model_User();
    $currentUser = $userModel->find($id)->current();
    $userForm->populate($currentUser->toArray());
    $this->view->form = $userForm;
}
```

Next you need to update the view script that Zend_Tool created for the update action. This is a very straightforward script that is nearly identical to the create action's view (see Listing 8-17).

Listing 8-17. The Update User View Script in application/views/scripts/user/update.phtml

```
<h2>Update user</h2>
<?php echo $this->form; ?>
```

Next, you'll process the form and update the user. This once again is very similar to the create action, except you will need to separate the updateUser() method (see Listing 8-18) and the updatePassword() method (see Listing 8-19) functions in the User model so you can update the password conditionally. Both of these methods will work like the createUser() method, updating values on a Zend_Db_Table_Row. The difference is that rather than creating a new row, you will find the row that matches the ID that is passed and update that.

Listing 8-18. The updateUser Method in application/user/models/User.php

```php
public function updateUser($id, $username, $firstName, $lastName, $role)
{
    // fetch the user's row
    $rowUser = $this->find($id)->current();

    if($rowUser) {
        // update the row values
        $rowUser->username = $username;
        $rowUser->first_name = $firstName;
        $rowUser->last_name = $lastName;
        $rowUser->role = $role;
        $rowUser->save();
        //return the updated user
        return $rowUser;
    }else{
        throw new Zend_Exception("User update failed.  User not found!");
    }
}
```

Listing 8-19. The updatePassword Method in application/user/models/User.php

```php
public function updatePassword($id, $password)
{
    // fetch the user's row
    $rowUser = $this->find($id)->current();

    if($rowUser) {
        //update the password
        $rowUser->password = md5($password);
        $rowUser->save();
    }else{
        throw new Zend_Exception("Password update failed.  User not found!");
    }
}
```

Now that the update user and password methods are created, you need to update the user controller's update action like you did the create function. When the form is posted back, you need to validate the data that was posted back and update the user if it passes, as shown in Listing 8-20.

Listing 8-20. The Updated Update Action in application/controllers/UserController.php

```php
public function updateAction ()
{
    $userForm = new Form_User();
    $userForm->setAction('/user/update');
    $userForm->removeElement('password');
    $userModel = new Model_User();
    if ($this->_request->isPost()) {
```

155

```
        if ($userForm->isValid($_POST)) {
            $userModel->updateUser(
                $userForm->getValue('id'),
                $userForm->getValue('username'),
                $userForm->getValue('first_name'),
                $userForm->getValue('last_name'),
                $userForm->getValue('role')
            );
            return $this->_forward('list');              }
    } else {
        $id = $this->_request->getParam('id');
        $currentUser = $userModel->find($id)->current();
        $userForm->populate($currentUser->toArray());
    }
    $this->view->form = $userForm;
}
```

Next you need to create a method to update the user's password. Create the password action using Zend_Tool, as shown in Listing 8-21.

Listing 8-21. Creating the User Password Action Using Zend_Tool

```
zf create action password user
```

The password action and view script will be nearly identical to the update action's. It will use the same form as the update action but will remove all the form controls except the ID and password. Then it will populate the user's ID, but not the password. On the postback, it will validate the post data and then call the User model's updatePassword() method, as shown in Listing 8-22.

Listing 8-22. The Password Action in application/controllers/UserController.php

```
public function passwordAction ()
{
    $passwordForm = new Form_User();
    $passwordForm->setAction('/user/password');
    $passwordForm->removeElement('first_name');
    $passwordForm->removeElement('last_name');
    $passwordForm->removeElement('username');
    $passwordForm->removeElement('role');
    $userModel = new Model_User();
    if ($this->_request->isPost()) {
        if ($passwordForm->isValid($_POST)) {
            $userModel->updatePassword(
                $passwordForm->getValue('id'),
                $passwordForm->getValue('password')
            );
            return $this->_forward('list');
        }
    } else {
        $id = $this->_request->getParam('id');
```

```
        $currentUser = $userModel->find($id)->current();
        $passwordForm->populate($currentUser->toArray());
    }
    $this->view->form = $passwordForm;
}
```

Now you have to update the views, so update the password view to render the form. You can copy the code from the update user view script; you need to update only the headline (see Listing 8-23) because you already updated the form in the controller.

Listing 8-23. The Updated Password View Script in application/views/scripts/user/password.phtml

```
<h2>Update user password</h2>
<?php echo $this->form; ?>
```

Once the password update method is implemented, you should update the update user form, adding a link to update the password. Note that you can fetch values from the form (in the view), as shown in Listing 8-24.

Listing 8-24. The Updated Update User Form in application/views/scripts/user/update.phtml

```
<h2>Update user</h2>
<?php echo $this->form; ?>
<p>
    <a href='/user/password/id/
                <?php echo $this->form->getElement('id')->getValue(); ?>'>
        Update Password
    </a>
</p>
```

Deleting Users

The final step in managing users is to create a method to delete them. This is the easiest part of the administration process since it does not require a form or view.

To do this, you need to create the delete user method in the User model. This method will try to find the user ID that is passed to it and will delete the row if it is successful, as shown in Listing 8-25.

Listing 8-25. The deleteUser *Method in* application/user/models/User.php

```
public function deleteUser($id)
{
    // fetch the user's row
    $rowUser = $this->find($id)->current();
    if($rowUser) {
        $rowUser->delete();
    }else{
        throw new Zend_Exception("Could not delete user.  User not found!");
    }
}
```

Then you need to add the delete action to the admin controller. You can do this with Zend_Tool, but since it does not require a view, it is probably simpler to type it. This action will simply fetch the ID that is passed in the URL and pass it to the User model to delete. Once the user is deleted, it redirects to the user list (Listing 8-26).

Listing 8-26. The Delete Action in application/controllers/UserController.php

```
public function deleteAction()
{

    $id = $this->_request->getParam('id');
    $userModel = new Model_User();
    $userModel->deleteUser($id);
    return $this->_forward('list');}
```

Note You will probably want to add a function to the user list that confirms that the administrator truly wants to delete the user. You can do this with JavaScript, but it is beyond the scope of this book.

Authenticating Users with Zend_Auth

You will use the Zend_Auth component to handle user authentication for this CMS project. It provides an authentication API that is implemented using authentication adapters. These adapters implement the Zend_Auth_Adapter_Interface interface, which standardize the authentication methods regardless of the method you employ.

The framework comes with a number of concrete auth adapters for common authentication methods that include:

- *Database table authentication*: This adapter authenticates against a database table.

- *Digest authentication*: Digest authentication is an improved method of HTTP authentication that does not transmit the password in plain text across the network.

- *LDAP authentication*: This method authenticates LDAP services.

- *Open ID*: Open ID authentication creates a single digital identity that can be used across the Internet.

You will use Zend_Auth_Adapter_DbTable since you're storing the site users and their credentials in a database table already.

Creating the User Landing Page

The default user page will provide a link to log in if the current user is not logged in; otherwise, it will display a link to log out. When you created the user controller with Zend_Tool, it added the default action, indexAction(), to the controller. You need to update this to load the current user and pass it to the view. You will need to fetch the current instance of Zend_Auth to do this. Note that because Zend_Auth implements the singleton pattern, there is only one instance at any given time. Once you have the Zend_Auth, use it to check whether an identity is set and pass this to the view, as shown in Listing 8-27.

Listing 8-27. *The indexAction() in application/controllers/UserController.php*

```php
public function indexAction()
{
    $auth = Zend_Auth::getInstance();

    if($auth->hasIdentity()) {
        $this->view->identity = $auth->getIdentity();
    }
}
```

Next you need to update the view script for the user controller's index action, as shown in Listing 8-28. This view script will need to check and see whether the identity has been set. If not, it will display a link to the login form. If there is an identity, it will display a logout link instead.

Listing 8-28. *The Default User Page in application/views/scripts/user/index.phtml*

```php
<h2>My Account</h2>
<?php if($this->identity == null) { ?>
    <p>To log in <a href='/user/login'>click here</a></p>
<?php }else{ ?>
    <p>Welcome back <?php echo $this->identity->first_name;?></p>
    <p>To log out <a href='/user/logout'>click here</a></p>
<?php } ?>
```

Creating the User Login

The user login action will require a couple of components; you need to create the login action that will render a login form. Then you need to authenticate the user with the username and password given. The first step is to create the login action. You can do this with Zend_Tool, as shown in Listing 8-29.

Listing 8-29. *Creating the User Login Action with Zend_Tool*

```
zf create action login user
```

Next you need to update the login action, loading the login form and passing it to the view to render. This is another example of a situation where you can reuse your user form—just remove all the elements except the username and password, as shown in Listing 8-30.

Listing 8-30. Loading the Login Form in application/controllers/UserController.php

```php
public function loginAction ()
{
    $userForm = new Form_User();
    $userForm->setAction('/user/login');
    $userForm->removeElement('first_name');
    $userForm->removeElement('last_name');
    $userForm->removeElement('role');
    $this->view->form = $userForm;
}
```

Then you need to update the view script to render the form, as shown in Listing 8-31. This script will need to render the login form the same way as you did with the create user form. It will also need to render one other thing, the login message. This is how you will tell the user whether their login attempt failed.

Listing 8-31. The User Login Form in application/views/scripts/user/login.phtml

```php
<h2>User Login</h2>
<p>To login to your account please enter your username and password below...</p>
<?php if($this->loginMessage) { ?>
<p><?php echo $this->loginMessage?></p>
<?php }
echo $this->form;
?>
```

Now you need to process this form and authenticate the user. This will take a few steps:

1. Confirm that the form is valid.

2. Get the Zend_Auth adapter. Pass this adapter the username and password the user entered, and then authenticate them.

3. If the user is valid, save the identity in the Zend_Auth storage, which will store the identity in a PHP session by default. Then send them to the welcome page. Otherwise, let them know the username or password they entered was invalid, and display the form again.

Listing 8-32 shows the updated login action.

Listing 8-32. The Updated loginAction() with User Authentication in
application/controllers/UserController.php

```php
public function loginAction ()
{
    $userForm = new Form_User();
    $userForm->setAction('/user/login');
    $userForm->removeElement('first_name');
    $userForm->removeElement('last_name');
    $userForm->removeElement('role');
```

```
    if ($this->_request->isPost() && $userForm->isValid($_POST)) {
        $data = $userForm->getValues();
        //set up the auth adapter
        // get the default db adapter
        $db = Zend_Db_Table::getDefaultAdapter();
        //create the auth adapter
        $authAdapter = new Zend_Auth_Adapter_DbTable($db, 'users',
            'username', 'password');
        //set the username and password
        $authAdapter->setIdentity($data['username']);
        $authAdapter->setCredential(md5($data['password']));
        //authenticate
        $result = $authAdapter->authenticate();
        if ($result->isValid()) {
            // store the username, first and last names of the user
            $auth = Zend_Auth::getInstance();
            $storage = $auth->getStorage();
            $storage->write($authAdapter->getResultRowObject(
                array('username' , 'first_name' , 'last_name', 'role')));
            return $this->_forward('index');        } else {
            $this->view->loginMessage = "Sorry, your username or
                password was incorrect";
        }
    }
    $this->view->form = $userForm;
}
```

Logging Users Out

Now that users can log in, you need to create the function for them to log out. This is very simple with Zend_Auth; you just clear the Zend_Auth instance's identity. Create the logoutAction(), which you can do with the Zend_Tool command in Listing 8-33.

Listing 8-33. Creating the User Logout Action with Zend_Tool

```
zf create action logout user
```

Next you need to fetch the current auth instance. Then clear the Zend_Auth identity using the clearIdentity() method, as shown in Listing 8-34.

Listing 8-34. The Logout Action in application/controllers/UserController.php

```
public function logoutAction ()
{
    $authAdapter = Zend_Auth::getInstance();
    $authAdapter->clearIdentity();
}
```

Then you just need to render a simple confirmation message for the user, letting them know that they did log out successfully. Add the message shown in Listing 8-35 to the logout view script.

Listing 8-35. The Logout Confirmation View in application/views/scripts/user/logout.phtml

```
<h2>User Logout</h2>
<p>You have successfully logged out...</p>
```

Adding User Controls to the Main CMS Interface

Now that the user authentication functions are set up, you need to make it easier for people to log in and log out. The user controller's index action displays these login/logout links; you only have to add it to the main site layout using the Zend_View action helper by adding the code in Listing 8-36 to the head of your site layout.

Listing 8-36. Loading the User Links into the Site Layout in application/layouts/scripts/layout.phtml

```
<?php
echo '<?xml version="1.0" encoding="UTF-8" ?>';
echo $this->doctype();
$this->layout()->nav = $this->action('render', 'menu', null,
    array('menu' => $this->mainMenuId));
$this->layout()->adminMenu = $this->action(
    'render', 'menu', null, array('menu' => $this->adminMenuId)
);
$this->layout()->userForm = $this->action('index', 'user');
?>

<html>
<head>
<meta http-equiv="Content-Type" content="text/html; charset=UTF-8" />
    <?php
    $this->loadSkin($this->skin);
    echo $this->headTitle();
    echo $this->headScript();
    echo $this->headLink();
    ?>
</head>

<body>
<div id="pageWrapper">
<div id="header">
<h1>Zend Framework CMS</h1>
</div>
<div id="nav">
        <?php
        echo $this->layout()->nav;
        ?> 
    </div>
```

```
<div id="sidebar">
<div id="subNav">
            <?php
            echo $this->layout()->subNav;
            ?> 
        </div>
<div id="adminMenu">
            <?php
            echo $this->layout()->adminMenu;
            ?> 
        </div>
<div id="userForm">
            <?php
            echo $this->layout()->userForm;
            ?> 
        </div>
</div>
<div id="main">
            <?php
            echo $this->layout()->content?> 
        </div>
<div id="footer">
<p><em>Powered by the Zend Framework</em></p>
</div>
</div>
</body>
</html>
```

Once this is loaded into the layout file, go to the home page of your site. You should now see the My Account section with a link to log in or log out on each page, as shown in Figure 8-3.

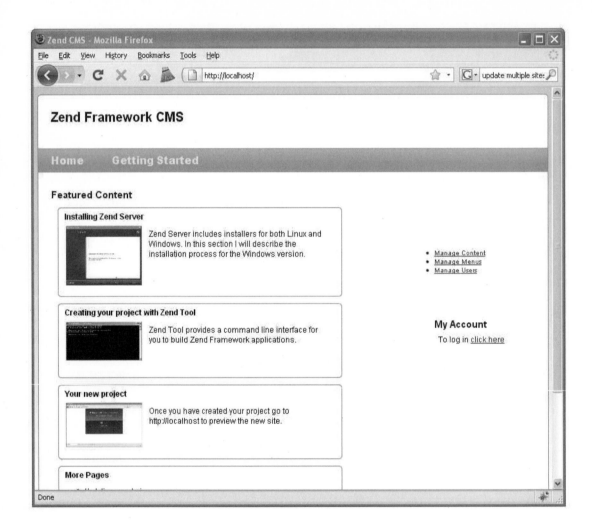

Figure 8-3. *The updated home page with login/logout links*

Controlling Access with Zend_Acl

Zend_Acl provides a simple and straightforward implementation of access control lists (ACLs). ACL consists of two lists:

- One list of resources (pages in your application)
- One list of roles (access roles, such as administrator)

Zend_Acl manages these lists as well as the relationships between the two. It then provides a method, isAllowed(), which you use to query the lists.

Using Zend_Acl

The first thing you need to do to use Zend_Acl is set up the roles. These roles represent the users in your application. You add these roles with the addRole() method, which you pass a new instance of Zend_Acl_Role.

These roles also support inheritance, so you more easily manage your user hierarchy. For example, you may have authors and publishers in a model. Say the authors have access to manage content but not publish it. Then the publishers are authors themselves, but they also have the authority to publish content to the site. In this example the publishers would extend the authors.

Next you set up the resources, which represent the modules, controllers, and actions in your application. You add resources to Zend_Acl using the add() method, to which you pass a new instance of Zend_Acl_Resource.

Now that you have the roles and resources set, you can define the ACL rules-in other words, who can access which resources. You do this with the allow() and deny() methods.

Once these rules are set up, your instance of ACL is ready to query, as shown in the simplistic example in Listing 8-37.

Listing 8-37. Sample Zend_Acl Usage

```
$acl = new Zend_Acl();

// create the user role
$acl->addRole(new Zend_Acl_Role('user'));

// create the admin role, which inherits all of the user's permissions
$acl->addRole(new Zend_Acl_Role('admin'), 'user');

// add a new resource
$acl->add(new Zend_Acl_Resource('cms'));

// set access rules
$acl->allow('admin', 'cms');
$acl->deny('guest', 'cms');

// query acl
// this will print 'allowed'echo $acl->isAllowed('admin', 'cms') ? 'allowed' : 'denied';
// this will print 'denied'
echo $acl->isAllowed('guest', 'cms') ? 'allowed' : 'denied';
```

Securing Your CMS Project

Once all the pieces are in place, securing a Zend Framework project is a straightforward process. This is because of, in a large part, the front controller pattern. All the page requests are processed by the controller, which means you can implement your security model in one place for the whole application.

The front controller uses a plug-in system to enable you to add this custom functionality without altering the core code library. Again, when the Bootstrap class initializes the front controller, it registers any plug-ins that are specified in the application.ini file.

In this example it makes sense to create a controller plugin to manage the access control. By doing this you are able to intercept the request and validate it before it is dispatched.

To get started, create a new folder in the CMS library named Controller and then a subfolder in Controller named Plugin. Add a new file to this folder named Acl.php. Next create a new class in this file named CMS_Controller_Plugin_Acl, which should extend Zend_Controller_Plugin_Abstract, as shown in Listing 8-38.

Listing 8-38. The ACL Controller Plug-in Class in /library/CMS/Controller/Plugin/Acl.php

```php
<?php
class CMS_Controller_Plugin_Acl extends Zend_Controller_Plugin_Abstract
{
}
```

Controller plug-ins respond to a number of events that have corresponding methods. In this case, you want to validate the user's permissions after the request has been processed but before it is dispatched. Create a new method in the ACL plug-in called preDispatch(), as shown in Listing 8-39.

Listing 8-39. The preDispatch Method in /library/CMS/Controller/Plugin/Acl.php

```php
public function preDispatch(Zend_Controller_Request_Abstract $request)
{
}
```

The first thing you need to do in this method is create an instance of Zend_Acl. Next you add the roles for each kind of CMS user as well as an unauthenticated guest role. This project will have three types of users:

- Guests: These are unauthenticated visitors

- Users: These are authenticated visitors. At this point you are not using this role, but it is nice to have. For example, you may want to enable logged in users to comment on content items. The logged in users will inherit all of the rights from guests.

- Administrator: The administrator manages the site. He has full access to the CMS.

Once you create the roles, you add a new resource for each of the controllers, as shown in Listing 8-40.

Listing 8-40. Adding ACL Roles and Resources in the preDispatch() Method of /library/CMS/Controller/Plugin/Acl.php

```php
// set up acl
$acl = new Zend_Acl();
```

```
// add the roles
$acl->addRole(new Zend_Acl_Role('guest'));
$acl->addRole(new Zend_Acl_Role('user'), 'guest');
$acl->addRole(new Zend_Acl_Role('administrator'), 'user');

// add the resources
$acl->add(new Zend_Acl_Resource('index'));
$acl->add(new Zend_Acl_Resource('error'));
$acl->add(new Zend_Acl_Resource('page'));
$acl->add(new Zend_Acl_Resource('menu'));
$acl->add(new Zend_Acl_Resource('menuitem'));
$acl->add(new Zend_Acl_Resource('user'));
```

Now you need to define the access rules. You can use two Zend_Acl methods to do this: allow() and deny(). You pass these methods three arguments: the role, the resources, and the permissions. See Listing 8-41 for an example of the rules for this CMS.

Note If you want to grant a user access to any resources, pass a null to the resource argument in the allow method. I did this for the administrators.

Listing 8-41. Setting the Access Rules in the preDispatch() Method of /library/CMS/Controller/Plugin/Acl.php

```
// set up the access rules
$acl->allow(null, array('index', 'error'));

// a guest can only read content and login
$acl->allow('guest', 'page', array('index', 'open'));
$acl->allow('guest', 'menu', array('render'));
$acl->allow('guest', 'user', array('login'));

// cms users can also work with content
$acl->allow('user', 'page', array('list', 'create', 'edit', 'delete'));

// administrators can do anything
$acl->allow('administrator', null);
```

With the ACL set up, you are ready to authenticate the user's request. First get the current user's role. If this is not set, then set the role to guest. Next, you query ACL, passing it the current role and request controller/action (see Listing 8-42). If there is an issue, you need to do one of two things. If the current user is a guest, then direct them to the login page. Otherwise, direct them to a "not authorized" error page, which you will create in one moment.

Listing 8-42. Querying ACL in the preDispatch() Method of /library/CMS/Controller/Plugin/Acl.php

```
// fetch the current user
$auth = Zend_Auth::getInstance();
if($auth->hasIdentity()) {
    $identity = $auth->getIdentity();
    $role = strtolower($identity->role);
}else{
    $role = 'guest';
}

$controller = $request->controller;
$action = $request->action;

if (!$acl->isAllowed($role, $controller, $action)) {
    if ($role == 'guest') {
        $request->setControllerName('user');
        $request->setActionName('login');
    } else {
        $request->setControllerName('error');
        $request->setActionName('noauth');
    }
}
```

Once this plugin is set up, you need to *register* the plugin with the front controller. You can do this by passing the plugin to the front controller application resource in the application.ini file (see Listing 8-43).

Listing 8-43. Registering the ACL Plugin with the Front Controller in
application/configs/application.ini

```
resources.frontController.plugins.acl = "CMS_Controller_Plugin_Acl"
```

Finally, you need to create the "not authorized" error page, which you can do with Zend_Tool. Execute the command in Listing 8-44 from your command line.

Listing 8-44. Creating the noauth Error Page with Zend_Tool

```
zf create action noauth error
```

Then update this page with an error message. This message should let the user know that they are not authorized to access the resource, as shown in Listing 8-45.

Listing 8-45. The noauth Error Page in application/views/scripts/error/noauth.phtml

```
<h2>Error: Not Authorized!</h2>
<p>Sorry, you are not authorized to access this resource.</p>
```

Summary

In this chapter, you learned how to manage security in a Zend Framework application. You started by creating the tools to manage the CMS users. Then you built the login and logout functionality, which you integrated with Zend_Auth. Once users could log in and out, you set up the access control plug-in using Zend_Acl and secured the CMS project.

CHAPTER 9

■■■

Searching and Sharing Content

CMSs make publishing to the Web significantly easier than traditional media, but that is only half the picture. One of the biggest advantages of web publishing is that you can enable your readers to search the content, be updated when the content changes, and even manipulate the data (with proper security measures, of course).

In this chapter, you will create a search engine for your CMS project using Zend_Search_Lucene. This framework component greatly simplifies indexing and searching site content. Then you will work with Zend_Feed, creating an RSS feed that your site visitors can subscribe to. Once this is done you will create an API for your CMS project that will allow other sites to access your content.

Working with the Lucene Search Engine

Zend Framework includes a version of the Lucene search engine that is so easy to use that I rarely build anything without it. Lucene is a full text search engine that was originally developed in Java and has been ported to a number of different languages. In this section you will use it to implement the default search engine for all of the content served by your CMS.

Before you get started, it makes sense to take a moment and go over what Zend_Search_Lucene does and does not do. It does provide a very straightforward way to build and search indexes of content. It does not automatically index your site like a search engine spider would. You have to manually add items to the index, but this extra step gives you a great deal of flexibility; you can build an index from virtually any data source.

Creating a Search Index

A Zend_Search_Lucene search index consists of documents, which in turn have fields containing searchable content. I often compare these to database tables, rows, and columns when explaining how to index content.

Creating a new search index is a simple process. Zend_Search_Lucene has a static `create` method, to which you pass the path to the directory where the index will be stored.

Documents and Fields

Zend_Search_Lucene uses documents as the container for your searchable content. To create a new document, you instantiate the Zend_Search_Lucene_Document class.

You add fields to the document using the `addField()` method. There are five types of fields: keyword, un-indexed, binary, text, and un-stored. Each of these types of fields has a combination of the following attributes:

- Stored fields: These fields are stored in the index and returned with the search results.

- Indexed: These fields are indexed and searchable.

- Tokenized: These fields are split into individual words.

- Binary: These fields can store binary data.

Table 9-1 describes the fields and their attributes.

Table 9-1. Attributes for Fields in Zend_Search_Lucene_Documents

Field Type	Stored	Indexed	Tokenized	Binary
Keyword	Yes	Yes	No	No
Unindexed	Yes	No	No	Yes
Binary	Yes	No	No	Yes
Text	Yes	Yes	Yes	No
Unstored	No	Yes	Yes	No

Implementing Site Search

The first step for adding the search functionality to your CMS is creating a new controller for it. You can create the controller using the **Zend_Tool** command in Listing 9-1.

Listing 9-1. Creating the Search Controller with Zend_Tool

```
zf create controller search
```

This command will create the search controller and its associated views.

Securing Site Search

Before you can access the search controller you need to add it to the ACL plug-in you created earlier. The first step is to add a resource to ACL for the search controller. So open `library/CMS/Controller/Plugin/Acl.php` and add a new resource for the search controller, as shown in Listing 9-2.

Listing 9-2. Adding the Resource for the Search Controller to library/CMS/Controller/Plugin/Acl.php

```
$acl->add(new Zend_Acl_Resource('search'));
```

The search controller will have two actions: the **build** action that will rebuild the search index and the index action that will perform a search and render the results. Everyone should be able to search the site, but only administrators should be able to rebuild the search index. Allow guests to access the index action, as shown in Listing 9-3.

Listing 9-3. Granting Guests Access to the Search Controller's Index Action in library/CMS/Controller/Plugin/Acl.php

```
$acl->allow('guest', 'search', array('index', 'search'));
```

Creating the Search Index

The next thing you need to do is create a folder for the index to reside in. Create a new folder in the `application` folder named `indexes`.

The Build Action

Next you need to create an action in the search controller that will build the search index. Create a new action in the search controller named **build**. You can do this using `Zend_Tool` with the command shown in Listing 9-4.

Listing 9-4. Creating the Build Action in the Search Controller with Zend_Tool

```
zf create action build search
```

Now open the search controller, and locate the **buildAction()** method. The first thing you need to do in the **buildAction()** method is to create the search index, which you can do with the `Zend_Search_Lucene::create()` method.

Once you have the index, you need to load it with the site content. Fetch all the pages from the **Model_Page()** model. Then create a **CMS_Content_Item_Page** object for each page. Next create a new document and add the page ID, headline, description, and content to it. Once the document is loaded add it to the index.

The final step is optimizing the index and passing data about the index to the view to report. You can see the completed buildAction() method in Listing 9-5.

Listing 9-5. Building the Search Index in the buildAction() of the SearchController in application/controllers/SearchController.php

```
public function buildAction()
{
    // create the index
    $index = Zend_Search_Lucene::create(APPLICATION_PATH . '/indexes');

    // fetch all of the current pages
    $mdlPage = new Model_Page();
    $currentPages = $mdlPage->fetchAll();
    if($currentPages->count() > 0) {
```

```
        // create a new search document for each page
        foreach ($currentPages as $p) {
            $page = new CMS_Content_Item_Page($p->id);
            $doc = new Zend_Search_Lucene_Document();
            // you use an unindexed field for the id because you want the id
            // to be included in the search results but not searchable
            $doc->addField(Zend_Search_Lucene_Field::unIndexed('page_id',
                $page->id));
            // you use text fields here because you want the content to be searchable
            // and to be returned in search results
            $doc->addField(Zend_Search_Lucene_Field::text('page_name',
                $page->name));
            $doc->addField(Zend_Search_Lucene_Field::text('page_headline',
                $page->headline));
            $doc->addField(Zend_Search_Lucene_Field::text('page_description',
                $page->description));
            $doc->addField(Zend_Search_Lucene_Field::text('page_content',
                $page->content));
            // add the document to the index
            $index->addDocument($doc);
        }
    }
    // optimize the index
    $index->optimize();
    // pass the view data for reporting
    $this->view->indexSize = $index->numDocs();
}
```

The Build Search View

Now that the **buildAction()** is complete, you need to update the view script that **Zend_Tool** created. This view script should display a headline, a confirmation message, and how many pages are in the index, as shown in Listing 9-6.

Listing 9-6. The Build View Script in application/views/scripts/search/build.phtml

```
<h2>Build Search Index</h2>
<p>You have successfully built the site search index.</p>
<p>Total pages indexed: <?php echo $this->indexSize; ?></p>
```

The final step for index management is to add a link to the admin menu. I created one with the label **Rebuild Search Index** that points to the **/search/build** URL.

Searching the Site

Now that you have an up-to-date search index, you are ready to wire up the site search.

The Search Form

The first thing you are going to need is a search form. Create a new file in **application/forms** named **SearchForm.php**. Then create a class in the **SearchForm.php** file named **Form_SearchForm**, which extends **Zend_Form**. **Zend_Form** runs a method called **init()** when it is constructed; this is where you build the form. Add a field for the search keywords and a submit button to the form, as shown in listing 9-7.

Listing 9-7. The Search Form in application/forms/Search.php

```php
<?php
class Form_SearchForm extends Zend_Form
{
    public function init()
    {
        // create new element
        $query = $this->createElement('text', 'query');
        // element options
        $query->setLabel('Keywords');
        $query->setRequired(true);
        $query->setAttrib('size',20);
        // add the element to the form
        $this->addElement($query);

        $submit = $this->createElement('submit', 'search');
        $submit->setLabel('Search Site');
        $submit->setDecorators(array('ViewHelper'));
        $this->addElement($submit);
    }
}
```

Adding the Search Form to the Site

Now you need to add the search form to the site. The search form should be on all the pages, so you need to add it to the layout file. Open the site layout script and locate the sidebar. Add the block that is in Listing 9-8 to the top of the sidebar.

Listing 9-8. The Search Form Block to Add to application/layouts/scripts/layout.phtml

```php
<div id='searchForm'>
        <h2>Search Site</h2>
        <?php
            $searchForm = new Form_Search();
            $searchForm->setAction('/search');
            echo $searchForm;
        ?>
        <br />
</div>
```

Processing a Search Request

The search form posts to the search controller's index action, which Zend_Tool created when it created the controller. Now you need to update this action to fetch the search keywords from the request object. Then you need to parse the query, which you can do automatically with the Zend_Search_Lucene_Search_QueryParser. Next open the search index and run the search. Finally, you pass the search results to the view to render, as shown in Listing 9-9.

Listing 9-9. The Updated indexAction() in application/controllers/SearchController.php

```php
public function indexAction()
{
    if($this->_request->isPost()) {
        $keywords = $this->_request->getParam('query');
        $query = Zend_Search_Lucene_Search_QueryParser::parse($keywords);
        $index = Zend_Search_Lucene::open(APPLICATION_PATH . '/indexes');
        $hits = $index->find($query);
        $this->view->results = $hits;
        $this->view->keywords = $keywords;
    }else{
        $this->view->results = null;
    }
}
```

Rendering Search Results

Now you need to update the view script that was created for the index action of the search controller. Start by adding a headline. Then check to confirm that there are search results to render. Next let the user know how many results their search returned, and render each result, as shown in Listing 9-10.

Listing 9-10. Rendering the Search Results in application/views/scripts/search/index.phtml

```php
<h2>Search Results</h2>
<?php if(is_array($this->results) && count($this->results) > 0) { ?>
<p>Your search for <em><?php echo $this->keywords; ?></em> returned <?php echo ↵
  count($this->results); ?> results.</p>
<?php foreach ($this->results as $result) { ?>
<h3><a href='/page/open/title/<?php echo $result->page_name; ?>'><?php echo ↵
  $result->page_headline; ?></a></h3>
<p><?php echo $result->page_description; ?></p>
<?php }} else {?>
<p>Your search did not return any results</p>
<?php }?>
```

Testing Site Search

Now you should be able to test the site search. First go to `http://localhost/search/build` to rebuild the search index. Enter a search term (or terms) in the search form and click **Submit Search**. You should see something like Figure 9-1.

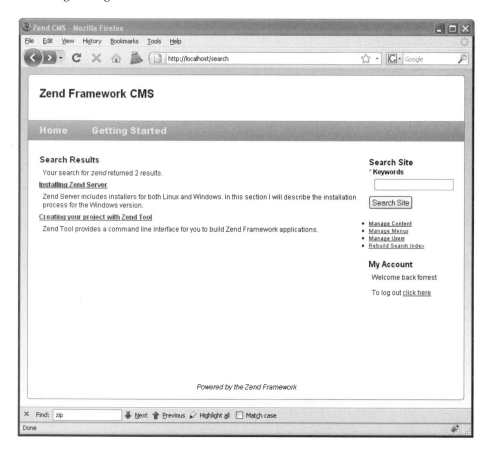

Figure 9-1. *Testing the site search*

Working with Zend Feed

Zend_Feed provides an interface for RSS and Atom feeds. It has methods to consume feeds as well as create them. In this section you will create an RSS feed for your CMS project that will publish a list of recent pages.

Creating the What's New Feed

The "what's new" feed will publish a list of the 10 newest pages. To get started, create a controller for the feeds called feed. You can do this with **Zend_Tool** using the command shown in Listing 9-11.

Listing 9-11. Creating the Feed Controller with Zend_Tool

```
zf create controller feed
```

Next create an action for the feed named **rss**. Listing 9-12 shows the **Zend_Tool** command to do this.

Listing 9-12. Creating the RSS Action in the Feed Controller with Zend_Tool

```
zf create action rss feed
```

Securing the Feeds

Now you'll update your ACL plug-in, granting everyone access to the feed controller. First create the feed resource (Listing 9-13).

Listing 9-13. Adding the Feed Resource to the ACL Plug-in in library/CMS/Controller/Plugin/Acl.php

```
$acl->add(new Zend_Acl_Resource('feed'));
```

Then grant guests access to the feed resource without specifying which actions they have access to, as shown in Listing 9-14.

Listing 9-14. Granting Guests Access to the Feed Resource to the ACL Plug-in in library/CMS/Controller/Plugin/Acl.php

```
$acl->allow('guest', 'feed');
```

Building and Rendering the Feed

Building a feed with Zend_Feed is a trivial task. You simply create an array with the feed data, add each entry, and then call the send() method, which sets the proper headers and renders the XML.

The first thing you need to do is open the feed controller and locate the RSS action. Then create the feed array and set the feed title, link, published timestamp, and character set (see Listing 9-15). You can add a number of other optional elements to the feed itself; refer to the Zend Framework web site for a complete list.

Listing 9-15. Creating the Feed Array in the RSS Action of the Feed Controller in application/controllers/FeedController.php

```
// build the feed array
$feedArray = array();

// the title and link are required
$feedArray['title'] = 'Recent Pages';
$feedArray['link'] = 'http://localhost';

// the published timestamp is optional
$feedArray['published'] = Zend_Date::now()->toString(Zend_Date::TIMESTAMP);
// the charset is required
$feedArray['charset'] = 'UTF8';
```

Now that you have created the feed array you need to fetch the recent pages and add each page to the feed. You do this by loading an array of entries and adding this to the feed array, as shown in Listing 9-16.

Listing 9-16. Adding the Recent Pages to the Feed in the RSS Action of the Feed Controller in application/controllers/FeedController.php

```
// first get the most recent pages
$mdlPage = new Model_Page();
$recentPages = $mdlPage->getRecentPages();

//add the entries
if(is_array($recentPages) && count($recentPages) > 0) {
    foreach ($recentPages as $page) {
        // create the entry
        $entry = array();
        $entry['guid'] = $page->id;
        $entry['title'] = $page->headline;
        $entry['link'] = 'http://localhost/page/open/title/' . $page->name;
        $entry['description'] = $page->description;
        $entry['content'] = $page->content;

        // add it to the feed
        $feedArray['entries'][] = $entry;
    }
}
```

Once you have built the feed array it is a trivial task to create the feed. You simply call the `Zend_Feed::importArray()` method, which you pass the array and the protocol to use. Then disable the layout and view renderer, and you are ready to send the feed, as shown in Listing 9-17.

Listing 9-17. Rendering the Feed in the RSS Action of the Feed Controller in application/controllers/FeedController.php

```
// create an RSS feed from the array
$feed = Zend_Feed::importArray($feedArray, 'rss');

// now send the feed
$this->_helper->viewRenderer->setNoRender();
$this->_helper->layout->disableLayout();
$feed->send();
```

Adding the Feed to the Site

Now that you have an RSS feed you need to let your site visitors know about it. Create a new box on the sidebar for the feed and add a link that points to **/feed/rss**, as shown in Listing 9-18.

Listing 9-18. The feed Block to Add to application/layouts/scripts/layout.phtml

```
<div id="feeds">
        <h2>Feeds</h2>
        <p><a href='/feed/rss'>Click Here</a> to subscribe to our RSS feed.</p>
</div>
```

Now when you click on this link your browser should load the RSS, as shown in Figure 9-2.

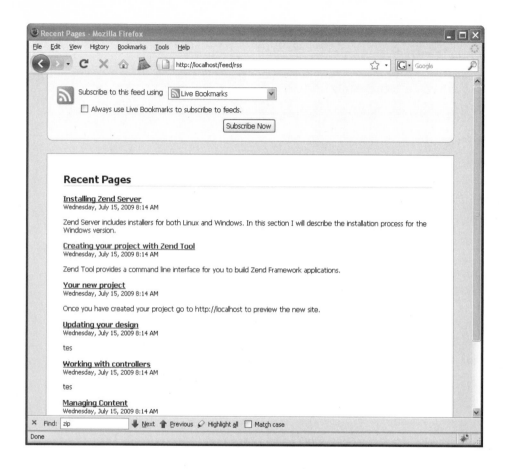

Figure 9-2. The "what's new" feed

Web Services and Zend Framework

Zend Framework includes a number of components that enable you to work with existing web services as well as create your own.

Working with Existing Services

Zend_Service provides a straightforward interface to a number of popular web services. These include Amazon, Flickr, Twitter, and Yahoo. The framework also features tight integration with a number of Google's services using the **Zend_Gdata** component.

Creating an API for your CMS with Zend REST

REST is arguably the simplest web service protocol. REST web services generally use arguments from URL parameters (a GET request), and they use POST to return the data.

The Zend_Rest component includes client and server functionality, making creating and interacting with REST web services a very straightforward process. In this section, you will create an API for the CMS project, which will enable other developers to interact with it directly. The API will contain methods to do the following:

- Search pages
- Create a new page
- Update an existing page
- Delete a page

The Base Class

The first thing you need to do is create the base class that will contain the methods that the service will expose. To get started create a file in the **library/CMS** folder named **Api.php**. Then create a class in the file named **CMS_Api**, as shown in Listing 9-19.

Listing 9-19. The Base CMS_Api Class in library/CMS/Api.php

```php
<?php
class CMS_Api
{
}
```

Securing the API

It is very important that you secure your CMS project's API prior to deploying it to a public server. You can do this in a number of ways, but for the time being, the **CMS_Api** class will handle authentication. It will do so by validating an API key, which you can hard-code for now.

Add a new protected method called **_validateKey()** to the **CMS_Api** class. This method should accept a single argument, the API key to validate. Validate the API key in the method and return true if it passes and false if not (see Listing 9-20).

Listing 9-20. The _validateKey() Method

```php
protected function _validateKey($apiKey)
{
    // this is for testing only
    if($apiKey == 'test') {
        return true;
    } else {
        return false;
    }
}
```

Searching Pages

The search method will be very similar to the index action of the search controller.

Create a new method in the CMS_Api class called **search()**. Then parse the query and run the search.

Once you have run the search you start building the response array. You can add whatever information you need to here, but for now it just needs to return the keywords you searched for, the number of hits, and the page for each hit. Now you return the response array for **Zend_Rest** to handle, as shown in Listing 9-21.

Listing 9-21. The search() Method of the CMS_Api Class in library/CMS/Api.php

```
public function search($apiKey, $keywords)
{
    if(!$this->_validateKey($apiKey)) {
        return array('error' => 'invalid api key', 'status' => false);
    }

    // fetch the index and run the search
    $query = Zend_Search_Lucene_Search_QueryParser::parse($keywords);
    $index = Zend_Search_Lucene::open(APPLICATION_PATH . '/indexes');
    $hits = $index->find($query);

    // build the response array
    if(is_array($hits) && count($hits) > 0) {
        $response['hits'] = count($hits);
        foreach ($hits as $page) {
            $pageObj = new CMS_Content_Item_Page($page->page_id);
            $response['results']['page_' . $page->page_id] = $pageObj->toArray();
        }
    } else {
        $response['hits'] = 0;
    }
}
```

Creating Pages

Add a new method to the CMS_Api class called **createPage()**. The create page method creates a new instance of the CMS_Content_Item_Page object, which it loads with the data that was passed to the method. It then saves the new page and converts the page object into an array to return, as shown in Listing 9-22.

Listing 9-22. The createPage() Method of the CMS_Api Class in library/CMS/Api.php

```
public function createPage($apiKey, $name, $headline, $description, $content)
{
    if(!$this->_validateKey($apiKey)) {
        return array('error' => 'invalid api key', 'status' => false);
    }
```

183

```
    // create a new page item
    $itemPage = new CMS_Content_Item_Page();
    $itemPage->name = $name;
    $itemPage->headline = $headline;
    $itemPage->description = $description;
    $itemPage->content = $content;

    // save the content item
    $itemPage->save();

    // return the page as an array, which Zend_Rest will convert into the XML response
    return $itemPage->toArray();
}
```

Updating Pages

Add a new method to the **CMS_Api** class named **updatePage()**. The update page method creates a new instance of the **CMS_Content_Item_Page** object, which it passes the page id to. The page object then loads the page and its content. Then it updates the page ID, saves the changes, and converts the page object into an array to return, as shown in Listing 9-23.

Listing 9-23. The updatePage() Method of the CMS_Api Class in library/CMS/Api.php

```
public function updatePage($apiKey, $id, $name, $headline, $description, $content)
{
    if(!$this->_validateKey($apiKey)) {
        return array('error' => 'invalid api key', 'status' => false);
    }

    // open the page
    $itemPage = new CMS_Content_Item_Page($id);

    // update it
    $itemPage->name = $name;
    $itemPage->headline = $headline;
    $itemPage->description = $description;
    $itemPage->content = $content;

    // save the content item
    $itemPage->save();

    // return the page as an array, which Zend_Rest will convert into the XML response
    return $itemPage->toArray();
}
```

Deleting Pages

Add a new method to the `CMS_Api` class called **deletePage()**. The delete page method will load a `CMS_Content_Item_Page` with the ID that was passed to it. If it is successful it needs to delete the page and return true; if not, then it returns false, as shown in Listing 9-24.

Listing 9-24. The deletePage() Method of the CMS_Api Class in library/CMS/Api.php

```php
public function deletePage($apiKey, $id)
{
    if(!$this->_validateKey($apiKey)) {
        return array('error' => 'invalid api key', 'status' => false);
    }

    // open the page
    $itemPage = new CMS_Content_Item_Page($id);
    if($itemPage) {
        $itemPage->delete();
        return true;
    }else{
        return false;
    }
}
```

Creating the API Server

Now that the underlying class is in place, it is very easy to create a REST server. Note that Zend Framework's REST service expects standard URL parameters, so the most straightforward way to create this server is to create a standalone file for it. Create a new file in the **public** directory called **Api.php**. Note that since this file exists on the file system, the **.htaccess** rewrite rules will map directly to it rather than rerouting the request to the **index.php** file.

The API file set up the application much like the **index.php** file, but it does not run the application. Instead, it creates a new instance of **Zend_Rest_Server**, which it passes the name of the **CMS_Api** class. Then it calls the server's **handle()** method, which does all the rest of the work for you, as shown in Listing 9-25.

Listing 9-25. Creating the REST Server in public/Api.php

```php
<?php
// Define path to application directory
defined('APPLICATION_PATH')
    || define('APPLICATION_PATH', realpath(dirname(__FILE__) . '/../application'));

// Define application environment
defined('APPLICATION_ENV')
    || define('APPLICATION_ENV', (getenv('APPLICATION_ENV') ? getenv('APPLICATION_ENV') : ↵
 'production'));
```

```
// Ensure library/ is on include_path
set_include_path(implode(PATH_SEPARATOR, array(
    realpath(APPLICATION_PATH . '/../library'),
    get_include_path(),
)));

/** Zend_Application */
require_once 'Zend/Application.php';

// Create application, bootstrap, and run
$application = new Zend_Application(
    APPLICATION_ENV,
    APPLICATION_PATH . '/configs/application.ini'
);
$application->bootstrap();

// now create the service
$server = new Zend_Rest_Server();
$server->setClass('CMS_Api');
$server->handle();
```

Testing the API

Now that the API is completed it is time to test it. Keep in mind that the API follows the REST protocol, rather than the standard Zend Framework URLs.

Testing Searching

Start by testing the search functionality. Point your browser to the following URL: http://localhost/Api.php?method=search&apiKey=test&keywords=zend. The API should return your search results as a neatly formed XML response, as shown in Listing 9-26.

Listing 9-26. The Search Method Response

```
<cms_api generator="zend" version="1.0">
      <search>
            <hits>1</hits>
            <results>
                  <page_{guid}>
                        <id>guid</id>
                        <name>name</name>
                        <headline>headline</headline>
                        <image>image path</image>
                        <description>description text</description>
                        <content>content text</content>
                        <parent_id>0</parent_id>
                  </page_{guid}>
            </results>
```

```
                <status>success</status>
        </search>
</cms_api>
```

Testing Creating a Page

Now test creating a page. Point your browser to
`http://localhost/Api.php?method=createPage&apiKey=test&name=test%20name&headline=test%20headli ne&description=test%20description&content=test%20content`. The API should create the new page, and return it as the response, as shown in Listing 9-27.

Listing 9-27. The Create Page Method Response

```
<cms_api generator="zend" version="1.0">
        <createpage>
                <id>12</id>
                <name>test name</name>
                <headline>test headline</headline>
                <image />
                <description>test description</description>
                <content>test content</content>
                <parent_id>0</parent_id>
                <status>success</status>
        </createpage>
</cms_api>
```

Updating the Page

Now update the page you just created. The update method is very similar to the create method, with the exception that you need to pass it the ID of the page to update. Point your browser to
`http://localhost/Api.php?method=updatePage&apiKey=test&id=12&name=new-name&headline=new-headline&description=new-description&content=new-content`. The API will update the page and return it as the response, as shown in Listing 9-28.

Listing 9-28. The Update Page Method Response

```
<cms_api generator="zend" version="1.0">
        <updatepage>
                <id>12</id>
                <name>new-name</name>
                <headline>new-headline</headline>
                <image />
                <description>new-description</description>
                <content>new-content</content>
                <parent_id>0</parent_id>
                <status>success</status>
        </updatepage>
</cms_api>
```

Deleting the Page

The final method to test is the delete method. You pass the delete method the id of the page to delete. Point your browser to `http://localhost/Api.php?method=deletePage&apiKey=test&id=12`. The API should delete the page and return a 1 as the response if it is deleted successfully, as shown in Listing 9-29.

Listing 9-29. The Delete Method Response

```
<cms_api generator="zend" version="1.0">
        <deletepage>
                <response>1</response>
                <status>success</status>
        </deletepage>
</cms_api>
```

Summary

In this chapter, you first learned the basics of how `Zend_Search_Lucene` works. You then added search functionality to the CMS project, including building the index, searching it, and rendering the results.

After adding search to the CMS, you learned about working with feeds and Zend Framework, adding a "what's new" feed to the project.

Once the feed was set up, you learned about working with web services and ZF, exposing some of the basic CMS functionality as a REST service.

CHAPTER 10

■ ■ ■

Extending Your CMS

The Zend Framework development team anticipated that programmers would need to build modular applications, creating the *conventional modular directory structure*. This structure enables you to create modules, which are essentially separate MVC applications, that you can use with different front controllers. In this chapter, you'll learn about working with them by creating a contact module.

The contact module will enable your site managers to publish and manage contact forms. This will be a very simple module but one that will be useful in many projects.

Note At the time of this writing, the Zend Tool Project has only basic support for modules. I use it to create the module's directory structure and then manually create the controllers and view scripts.

Creating the Module

To get started, create the contact module using the `Zend Tool Project`'s `create module` command, as shown in Listing 10-1. This will create the module directory and the required subdirectories.

Listing 10-1. Creating the Contact Module with Zend Tool Project

```
zf create module contact
```

Now you need to create the contact controllers and views manually. First create the index controller. Add a new file to the **application/modules/contact/controllers** directory named **IndexController.php**. Open this file, and add the controller class. Note that the class names of the module controllers are prepended with the module namespace, so in this case the controller class name should be `Contact_IndexController`. Add an empty `indexAction()` method to this controller, as shown in Listing 10-2.

Listing 10-2. The Contact Module's IndexController in
application/modules/contact/controllers/IndexController.php

```php
<?php
class Contact_IndexController extends Zend_Controller_Action
```

```
{
    public function indexAction()
    {

    }
}
```

Next you need to add a directory to the module's view directory for the index controller's views named `index`. Then add a new file to this directory named `index.phtml`. Add a headline to the page for now, as shown in Listing 10-3. You will add the actual contact form to this page shortly.

Listing 10-3. The Default Contact Module Page in

application/modules/contact/views/scripts/index/index.phtml

```
<h2>Contact Us</h2>
```

Configuring Your Application to Load Modules

Now that the contact module is created, you need to configure your application to load it. This requires two things; you need to update the main application configuration file and create a bootstrap file for the contact module.

To get started, open the configuration file (`application/configs/application.ini`). First set the front controller's module directory to `modules`. Once this is set, the front controller will automatically load each of the modules that are in this directory. Next set the module resource to an empty array. Then you need to override the setting you added earlier, where you set the default controller to `page`. Set this back to `index`. Listing 10-4 shows the three lines you need to add.

Listing 10-4. The Updates You Need to Make to application/configs/application.ini

```
resources.frontController.moduleDirectory = APPLICATION_PATH "/modules"
resources.modules[] = ""
contact.resources.frontController.defaultControllerName = "index"
```

The last step of configuring your module is to bootstrap it. If your module has a file named `Bootstrap.php` in its root with a class named `{Module}_Bootstrap`, then `Zend_Application` will use this file to bootstrap your module. In the contact form's case, there is not a lot of custom configuration required; it needs only to reset the `defaultControllerName`. It will do this automatically since you set it in the configuration file.

Create a new file in the root of your contact module named `Bootstrap.php`. Add a class to this file named `Contact_Bootstrap`, which should extend `Zend_Application_Module_Bootstrap`, as shown in Listing 10-5.

Listing 10-5. The Contact Module Bootstrap File in application/modules/contact/Bootstrap.php

```
<?php
class Contact_Bootstrap extends Zend_Application_Module_Bootstrap
{}
```

Once this file is in place, you should be able to point your browser to `http://localhost/contact` and see the index page of the contact module.

Rendering the Contact Form

Now that the contact module is wired up, you are ready to construct the contact form. Create a new directory in the contact module named `forms`. Then create a new file in this directory named `Contact.php`. The module resources (forms and models) will be automatically loaded if you follow the module namespace convention like the controller class; the contact form class will be called `Contact_Form_Contact`. Add this class to the `Contact.php` file.

The contact form will need four fields: the person's name, their e-mail address, the subject, and the message. All of the fields are required. You will also need to validate that the e-mail address is valid. Listing 10-6 shows the completed form.

Listing 10-6. The Contact Form in application/modules/contact/forms/Contact.php

```php
<?php
class Contact_Form_Contact extends Zend_Form
{
    public function init()
    {
        // create new element
        $name = $this->createElement('text', 'name');
        // element options
        $name->setLabel('Enter your name:');
        $name->setRequired(TRUE);
        $name->setAttrib('size',40);
        // add the element to the form
        $this->addElement($name);

        // create new element
        $email = $this->createElement('text', 'email');
        // element options
        $email->setLabel('Enter your email address:');
        $email->setRequired(TRUE);
        $email->setAttrib('size',40);
        $email->addValidator('EmailAddress');
        $email->addErrorMessage('Invalid email address!');
        // add the element to the form
        $this->addElement($email);

        // create new element
        $subject = $this->createElement('text', 'subject');
        // element options
        $subject->setLabel('Subject: ');
        $subject->setRequired(TRUE);
        $subject->setAttrib('size',60);
        // add the element to the form
```

```
    $this->addElement($subject);

    // create new element
    $message = $this->createElement('textarea', 'message');
    // element options
    $message->setLabel('Message:');
    $message->setRequired(TRUE);
    $message->setAttrib('cols',50);
    $message->setAttrib('rows',12);
    // add the element to the form
    $this->addElement($message);

    $submit = $this->addElement('submit', 'submit',
        array('label' => 'Send Message'));
    }
}
```

Now you need to load the form in the contact module's index controller. Open the file, and update the indexAction() method; first create an instance of the form, then set the action and method, and finally pass it to the view to render, as shown in Listing 10-7.

Listing 10-7. The Updated indexAction() in

application/modules/contact/controllers/IndexController.php

```
public function indexAction()
{
    $frmContact = new Contact_Form_Contact();
    $frmContact->setAction('/contact');
    $frmContact->setMethod('post');
    $this->view->form = $frmContact;
}
```

Then you simply need to update the view script to render the form, as shown in Listing 1087.

Listing 10-8. Rendering the Contact Form in

application/modules/contact/views/scripts/index/index.phtml

```
<h2>Contact Us</h2>
<p>To send us a message please complete the form below and click Send Message.</p>
<?php echo $this->form; ?>
```

Once you have updated the view script, point your browser to http://localhost/contact, and you should see the contact form in Figure 10-1.

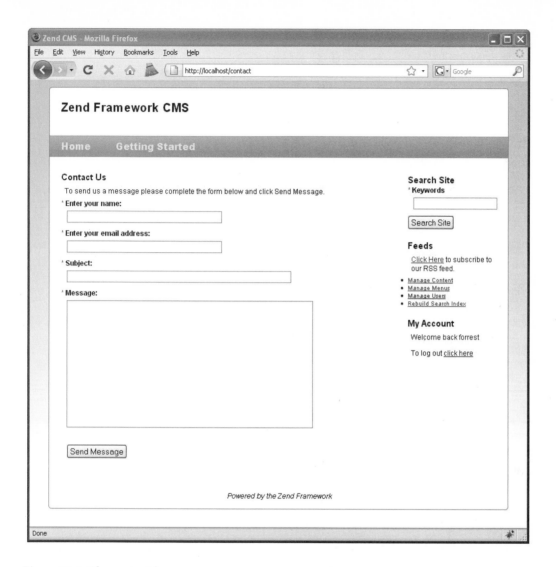

Figure 10-1. The contact form

Processing the Contact Form

Now that the form is completed, you need to update the `indexAction()` method of the contact index controller again to process the form submission. This process will be very similar to the other forms that you have worked with. First you need to check and see whether the request method is POST, which means that the form has been posted back. Next you need to load the form with the POST data and confirm that it is valid (as shown in Listing 10-9). If it is valid, then you can send the message.

Listing 10-9. The Updated Index Action in

application/modules/contact/controllers/IndexController.php

```
public function indexAction()
{
    $frmContact = new Contact_Form_Contact();
    if($this->_request->isPost() && $frmContact->isValid($_POST)) {
        //send the message
    }
    $frmContact->setAction('/contact');
    $frmContact->setMethod('post');
    $this->view->form = $frmContact;
}
```

Note that I just added a placeholder where you are going to send the message. I will go over that process next.

Sending Mail with Zend_Mail

The `Zend_Mail` component gives you the capability to send e-mail messages from your project. You can send either plain-text messages or rich HTML messages. You have a number of options regarding the transport method you use. I generally use the default sendmail client, but you can use SMTP if you want to route your mail through a different server.

In this example, I'll show how to send an HTML message through the sendmail client, but feel free to modify this if necessary.

Creating the Mail Template

The first thing you need to do is format the message as HTML. The easiest way to do this is to create a template that you pass the data to. The template is just a standard `Zend_View` script, with placeholders for the sender's contact information and the message. Create a new directory in `application/modules/contact/views/scripts` named `templates`, and then add a file to this named `default.phtml`. Add the placeholders to this script, as shown in Listing 10-10.

Listing 10-10. The E-mail Template in

application/modules/contact/views/scripts/templates/default.phtml

```
<h1>Contact Form Submission</h1>
<p>You received a new contact form submission from:</p>
<ul>
    <li>Name: <?php echo $this->name; ?></li>
    <li>Email Address: <?php echo $this->email; ?></li>
</ul>
<h2>Message</h2>
<h3><?php echo $this->subject; ?></h3>
<p><?php echo $this->message; ?></p>
```

Rendering and Sending the HTML Message

Now that you have the pieces in place, you are ready to build and send the message.

■ **Note** This will throw an error if you do not have mail configured on your testing server. You can alternatively use SMTP transport rather than defaulting to the local server to test this mail functionality. I will explain how to do this later in the chapter.

The first thing you need to do is load the data from the form. Although this is not technically necessary, I find that fetching these values and setting local variables makes the code easier to read.

The next step is loading the HTML template. You do this with the Zend_View Partial helper, which you pass the array of form data to.

Once the message is built, you are ready to send it. The PHP mail() function is very simple but can get complicated when you need to send multipart messages (such as this one), add attachments, and so on. The Zend_Mail component builds onto this basic functionality, providing rich e-mail functionality without manual configuration.

To get started with Zend_Mail, you need to create an instance of the class. Then you set the message subject and to and from fields.

Now you set the body of the message. When you send an HTML email, it is very important to also send a text-only version of the message; there are still some mail clients that don't support HTML email. Zend_Mail includes two methods for setting the body of the message: setBodyText(), which sets the text-only version, and setBodyHtml(), which sets the HTML version. Zend_Mail automatically sets the MIME content type to test/html and multipart/alternative if you use both methods on one message.

Once the message is finished, you send it using the send() method. Finally, you need to pass a flag to the view to let it know whether the message was sent or not, as shown in Listing 10-11.

Listing 10-11. The Completed Contact Controller Index Action in the Updated Index Action in application/modules/contact/controllers/IndexController.php

```php
public function indexAction()
{
    $frmContact = new Contact_Form_Contact();
    if($this->_request->isPost() && $frmContact->isValid($_POST)) {
        // get the posted data
        $sender = $frmContact->getValue('name');
        $email = $frmContact->getValue('email');
        $subject = $frmContact->getValue('subject');
        $message = $frmContact->getValue('message');

        // load the template
        $htmlMessage = $this->view->partial(
            'templates/default.phtml',
            $frmContact->getValues()
        );
```

```
        $mail = new Zend_Mail();
        // set the subject
        $mail->setSubject($subject);
        // set the message's from address to the person who submitted the form
        $mail->setFrom($email, $sender);
        // for the sake of this example you can hardcode the recipient
        $mail->addTo('webmaster@somedomain.com', 'webmaster');
        // it is important to provide a text only version in
        // addition to the html message
        $mail->setBodyHtml($htmlMessage);
        $mail->setBodyText($message);
        //send the message
        $result = $mail->send();
        // inform the view with the status
        $this->view->messageProcessed = true;
        if($result) {
            $this->view->sendError = false;
        } else {
            $this->view->sendError = true;
        }
    }
    $frmContact->setAction('/contact');
    $frmContact->setMethod('post');
    $this->view->form = $frmContact;
}
```

The Confirmation Message

Now that you have processed the form, you need to let the user know whether the message was sent or whether issues were encountered. In Listing 10-11, you set flags in the view to notify the script of the status. Next you need to update the view script to display the confirmation or error message (Listing 10-12).

Listing 10-12. The Updated Contact Form in

application/modules/contact/views/scripts/index/index.phtml

```
<h2>Contact Us</h2>
<?php if($this->messageProcessed && $this->sendError) { ?>
    <p>Sorry there was an error sending your message. Please contact↵
 support@somedomain.com for more help.</p>
<?php } elseif ($this->messageProcessed &! $this->sendError) {?>
    <p>Thank you for contacting us. We will be in touch soon.</p>
<?php } else { ?>
    <p>To send us a message please complete the form below
        and click Send Message.</p>
    <?php echo $this->form;
}
```

Securing the Form with Captcha

You will almost be guaranteed to get some spam when you publish a contact form on your site. You can minimize this in a number of ways (such as asking a simple mathematical question), but CAPTCHA (Completely Automated Public Turing test to tell Computers and Humans Apart) is the most effective at the time of this writing. It authenticates that a real person is submitting the form rather than an automated process. It does this by requiring the user to perform some challenge task, such as typing the letters of a graphical piece of text, which is difficult (but not impossible) for an automated process to do.

Zend_Captcha includes a number of back-end adapters that can generate CAPTCHA for your program:

- Zend_Captcha_Word: This is the main base adapter.

- Zend_Captcha_Dumb: This is a simple adapter that produces a string that you need to type backward.

- Zend_Captcha_Figlet: This adapter produces a Figlet that the user must type exactly.

- Zend_Captcha_Image: This adapter converts a string to an image with a skewed font.

- Zend_Captcha_Recaptcha: This adapter uses the Recaptcha service to generate the CAPTCHA.

I have used several of the adapters, but I really like the Recaptcha service. It is a web project that is attempting to digitize literature that was written prior to the digital revolution. It does this by photographically scanning the works and then transforming it into text using "optical character recognition" software. The issue is that this software is not perfect, so the Recaptcha service sends the text that it cannot translate to humans to decipher. You get a simple and effective CAPTCHA service while helping this project.

To get started using the Recaptcha service, you need to sign up on its site (http://recaptcha.net) for an API key. Once you have this key, integrating the service with your form is a trivial task. Zend_Form has a CAPTCHA form element that handles the rendering and validation for you. Add this element to your form, configuring it as is demonstrated in Listing 10-13.

Listing 10-13. The CAPTCHA Form Control in application/modules/contact/forms/Contact.php

```
// configure the captcha service
$privateKey = 'your private key';
$publicKey = 'your public key';
$recaptcha = new Zend_Service_ReCaptcha($publicKey, $privateKey);

// create the captcha control
$captcha = new Zend_Form_Element_Captcha('captcha',
    array('captcha'      => 'ReCaptcha',
        'captchaOptions' => array('captcha' => 'ReCaptcha', 'service' => $recaptcha)));

// add captcha to the form
$this->addElement($captcha);
```

Now if you point your browser to the contact form (http://localhost/contact), you should see the Recaptcha control, as in Figure 10-2.

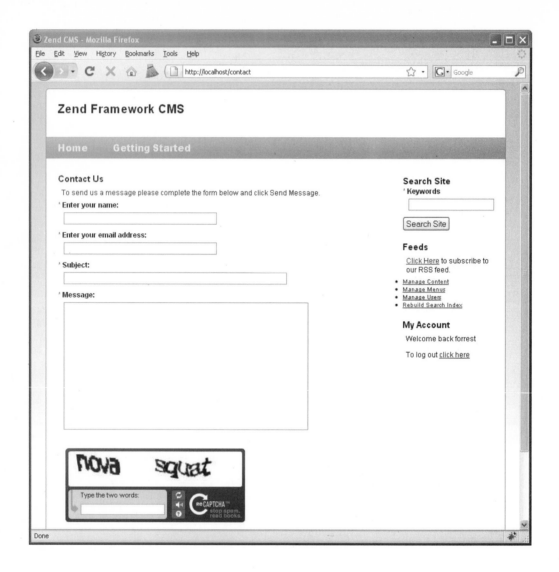

Figure 10-2. The contact form, secured with the Recaptcha form element

Using SMTP Mail Transport

There are many situations where you may not want to use the default mail server. A few examples include when you are working on a development server that does not have a mail server configured and when your site has a large volume of messages that you do not want bogging down your web server. SMTP mail transport enables you to send mail through a remote server.

To configure Zend_Mail to use SMTP transport, you first have to create a new instance of Zend_Mail_Transport_Smtp, which you configure with the address to the mail server and your user credentials. Listing 10-14 demonstrates how to update the mail method in the indexAction() to use SMTP transport.

Listing 10-14. Updating the Mail Method to Use SMTP Transport in the indexAction() of

application/modules/contact/controllers/IndexController.php

```
$mail = new Zend_Mail();
// configure and create the SMTP connection
$config = array('auth' => 'login',
    'username' => 'myusername',
    'password' => 'password');

$transport = new Zend_Mail_Transport_Smtp('mail.server.com', $config);

// set the subject
$mail->setSubject($subject);
// set the message's from address to the person who submitted the form
$mail->setFrom($email, $sender);
// for the sake of this example you can hardcode the recipient
$mail->addTo('webmaster@somedomain.com', 'webmaster');
// it is important to provide a text only version in addition to the html message
$mail->setBodyHtml($htmlMessage);
$mail->setBodyText($message);
//send the message, now using SMTP transport
$result = $mail->send($transport);
```

File Attachments

You may want to enable file attachments on your contact form in certain circumstances. For example, your users might need to upload a screenshot if the form is being used for technical support.

Attaching files to your contact form messages is a two-step process; first you need to upload the file from the user's desktop to the server, and then you need to attach the file to the message. A number of other things need to be done behind the scenes, such as setting the MIME type, but Zend_Mail handles that for you.

Uploading the File

The first thing you need to do is update the contact form and indexAction() to enable the users to upload files.

■ **Caution** The file element requires a little more configuration than many of the other elements; allowing a site visitor to upload a file onto your server is not something to take lightly!

199

Start by creating a new directory for the file uploads named uploads. This directory should be in the root of your project because these files should never be publicly accessible.

Then add a new file element to the contact form beneath the subject element, setting the upload destination to the upload directory you just created.

The next step is validating the upload. Note that for this example I limited uploads to image files, but you can add any file types you need to allow. Add the following validators to your file element:

- *Count*: Ensures that only one file is uploaded

- *Size*: Sets a reasonable limit to the file size, in this case 100KB

- *Extension*: Ensures that only allowed file types can be uploaded

The final step is setting the enctype attribute of the form to multipart/form-data so it accepts file uploads. Listing 10-14 shows the complete element.

Listing 10-14. Creating the File Upload Control in application/modules/contact/forms/Contact.php

```
// create new element
$attachment = $this->createElement('file', 'attachment');
// element options
$attachment->setLabel('Attach a file');
$attachment->setRequired(FALSE);
// specify the path to the upload folder. this should not be publicly accessible!
$attachment->setDestination(APPLICATION_PATH . '/../uploads');
// ensure that only 1 file is uploaded
$attachment->addValidator('Count', false, 1);
// limit to 100K
$attachment->addValidator('Size', false, 102400);
// only allow images to be uploaded
$attachment->addValidator('Extension', false, 'jpg,png,gif');
// add the element to the form
$this->addElement($attachment);
// set the enctype attribute for the form so it can upload files
$this->setAttrib('enctype', 'multipart/form-data');
```

Now if you point your browser to the contact form (http://localhost/contact), you should see the file control, as in Figure 10-3.

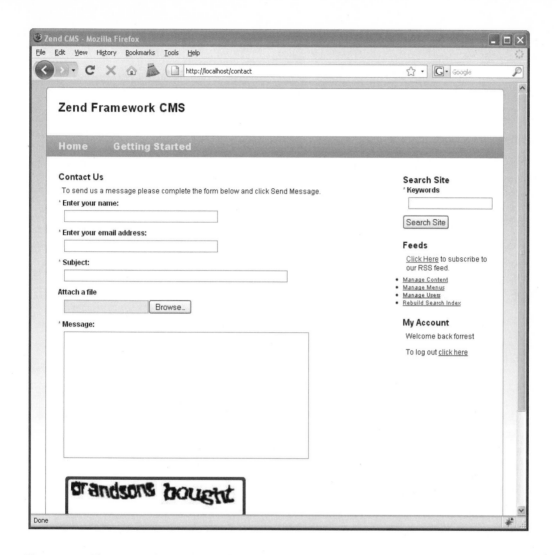

Figure 10-3. The contact form with the file upload control

Attaching the File to Your Message

Now you need to process the uploaded file and attach it to the message. Zend_Form_Element_File handles the file upload process, so the first thing you need to do is get the attachment element. Then confirm that a file was uploaded since this is an optional field. The next step is fetching the filename from the attachment element and loading the file into a binary stream. Once you have this data, you can create a new attachment using the Zend_Mail createAttachment() method. Zend_Mail handles the rest of the process.

■ **Note** In a production environment, you should create a method to clean the uploaded files, as they can take up a lot of hard drive space if left unchecked.

Listing 10-15. Updating the Mail Method to Enable File Attachments in the indexAction() of application/modules/contact/controllers/IndexController.php

```
$mail = new Zend_Mail();
// configure and create the SMTP connection
$config = array('auth' => 'login',
    'username' => 'myusername',
    'password' => 'password');

$transport = new Zend_Mail_Transport_Smtp('mail.server.com', $config);

// set the subject
$mail->setSubject($subject);
// set the message's from address to the person who submitted the form
$mail->setFrom($email, $sender);
// for the sake of this example you can hardcode the recipient
$mail->addTo('webmaster@somedomain.com', 'webmaster');
// add the file attachment
$fileControl = $frmContact->getElement('attachment');
if($fileControl->isUploaded()) {
    $attachmentName = $fileControl->getFileName();
    $fileStream = file_get_contents($attachmentName);
    // create the attachment
    $attachment = $mail->createAttachment($fileStream);
    $attachment->filename = basename($attachmentName);
}
// it is important to provide a text only version in addition to the html message
$mail->setBodyHtml($htmlMessage);
$mail->setBodyText($message);
//send the message, now using SMTP transport
$result = $mail->send($transport);
```

Summary

In this chapter, you learned how to extend a Zend Framework project by adding modules to the project. After this brief overview, you created a new contact module, which served as a good example of a very common addition to dynamic web sites. While you built this module, you also learned how to create and send e-mail messages with `Zend_Mail`, including some of the more advanced features such as using SMTP transport and handling file attachments.

■■■

CHAPTER 11

Advanced Topics

Over the course of this book, you have learned how to develop Zend Framework applications, working with many of the most commonly used components. In this chapter, I'll discuss some other components that will likely find a place in your day-to-day work.

Performance Tuning

When you are rapidly developing dynamic web applications, it is far too easy to get caught up in functionality at the expense of performance—or performance at the expense of functionality.

I often run into a common issue when I create a method in a model that runs a couple of queries and returns some sort of aggregated result. This in itself is not an issue. The issue comes up when you become complacent with regard to the number of queries that you are running behind the method call or do not consider how the system will behave under heavy load.

About Zend_Db_Profiler

The first thing I do when I notice performance issues is to enable `Zend_Db_Profiler`. It provides a wealth of information about the queries that are being run without adding debugging code to your project classes. Having this information at hand makes it much easier to locate and remedy bottlenecks.

■ **Note** One additional benefit of profiling `Zend_Db` is getting to see all the SQL that `Zend_Db` generates. I am a bit of a control freak and like to know what is going on behind the scenes!

Testing Your Application

Configuring your application to use the database profiler is a trivial task. You simply set the database parameter profiler to `true` in the `application.ini` config file in the development section, as shown in Listing 11-1. By adding this to the development section, the profiler will be enabled locally but will not be in the production environment.

Listing 11-1. Turning On the db Profiler in application/configs/application.ini

```
resources.db.params.profiler = true
```

Once the profiler is turned on, you need a way to view the data. You could add this directly to the main layout file, but you will probably need to do this in every project that uses `Zend_Db`, so it makes sense to create a view script to render the profiling results. By doing this, you will be able to drop this file into any other application that uses the profiler.

Creating the Profiler View Script

To get started, create a new view directory in `application/views/scripts` named `util`. Then create a new file named `profiler.phtml` in the `util` directory.

The first thing the profiler view script needs to do is fetch the current database adapter and determine whether the profiler is enabled. If it is not enabled, then the script does nothing. If it is, it generates a table with the profiling information, as shown in Listing 11-2.

Listing 11-2. The Profiler View Script in `application/views/scripts/util/profiler.php`

```php
<?php
// get the default db adapter
$db = Zend_Db_Table::getDefaultAdapter();
$profiler = $db->getProfiler();
if($profiler->getEnabled() && $profiler->getTotalNumQueries() > 0) { ?>
<div style='text-align:center'>
<h2>Database Profiling Report</h2>
    <p>Total queries executed: <?php echo $profiler->getTotalNumQueries()?></p>
    <p>Total elapsed time: <?php echo $profiler->getTotalElapsedSecs()?></p>
</div>
<table class='spreadsheet' cellpadding='0' cellspacing='0' style='margin:10px auto'>
    <thead>
        <tr>
            <th>#</th>
            <th>Query</th>
            <th>Time</th>
        </tr>
    </thead>
    <tbody>
<?php foreach ($profiler->getQueryProfiles() as $queryNumber => $query) { ?>
    <tr>
        <td>(<?php echo $queryNumber + 1?>)</td>
        <td><?php echo $query->getQuery();?></td>
        <td><?php echo $query->getElapsedSecs();?></td>
    </tr>
<?php }?>
    </tbody>
</table>
<?php }?>
```

Adding the Profiler Script to the Site

Now you need to render this file in the main layout script. This will enable you to profile every page on the site with no additional effort.

You render this script as you would any other view script with one additional consideration; the view renderer helper automatically sets the view script path to the current module's view directory. Zend_View will throw an exception when you try to view a module page, such as http://localhost/contact, since there is probably no util/profiler.phtml file in its view directory.

This is easy to fix—you just add the script path before you render it. You don't need to worry about any conflicts with the module scripts since the module's action controller has already rendered its response by the time the layout file is rendered.

Update the main site layout file (application/layouts/scripts/layout.phtml) to render the profiler script after the closing </body> tag. First add the script path to the main application view directory, and then render the profiler.phtml file, as shown in Listing 11-3.

Listing 11-3. Rendering the Profiler Script in application/layouts/scripts/layout.phtml

```
</body>
<?php
    $this->addScriptPath(APPLICATION_PATH . '/views/scripts');
    echo $this->render('util/profiler.phtml');
```

Now when you load any page, you should see the database profiling report at the bottom of the page, as shown in Figure 11-1.

Database Profiling Report

Total queries executed: 15

Total elapsed time: 0.011603116989136

#	Query	Time
(1)	connect	0.0011670589447021
(2)	DESCRIBE `pages`	0.0013909339904785
(3)	SELECT `pages`.* FROM `pages` WHERE (name = 'Installing Zend Server') LIMIT 1	0.00041699409484863
(4)	DESCRIBE `pages`	0.0011181831359863
(5)	SELECT `pages`.* FROM `pages` WHERE (((`pages`.`id` = 5)))	0.00032520294189453
(6)	DESCRIBE `content_nodes`	0.0012180805206299
(7)	SELECT `content_nodes`.* FROM `content_nodes` WHERE (`page_id` = 5)	0.0003509521484375
(8)	DESCRIBE `menu_items`	0.0012729167938232
(9)	SELECT `menu_items`.* FROM `menu_items` WHERE (menu_id = 3) ORDER BY `position` ASC	0.00031900405883789
(10)	DESCRIBE `pages`	0.0010108947753906
(11)	SELECT `pages`.* FROM `pages` WHERE (((`pages`.`id` = 5)))	0.00022411346435547
(12)	DESCRIBE `content_nodes`	0.00096702575683594
(13)	SELECT `content_nodes`.* FROM `content_nodes` WHERE (`page_id` = 5)	0.00035595893859863
(14)	DESCRIBE `menu_items`	0.001140832901001
(15)	SELECT `menu_items`.* FROM `menu_items` WHERE (menu_id = 5) ORDER BY `position` ASC	0.00032496452331543

Figure 11-1. The database profiling report

This information reveals an issue with the application; a few queries are duplicated several times. Looking back at the code, this makes sense; when you refactored the page controller to use SEO-friendly URLs, you added a new query that fetches the page row by the name. Then it passes the row `id` to the CMS_Content_Item_Page. The issue is the fact that the CMS_Content_Item_Page class then takes the ID and fetches the same information again. Time to refactor!

Optimizing the CMS_Content_Item_Page Class

The CMS_Content_Item_Page class loads the page based on the ID that you pass the constructor. This worked before you refactored for the SEO-friendly URLs but now adds an extra, unnecessary query.

One solution to this issue is to update the CMS_Content_Item_Page class so you have the option to pass it a Zend_Db_Table_Row. To do this, you need to update two methods in the abstract CMS_Content_Item_Abstract class: the **constructor** method and the loadPageObject() method.

The **constructor** method was set up to pass the page as an integer. You need to update this function to enable it to pass the page to the **loadPageMethod()** method as an object or an integer, as shown in Listing 11-4.

Listing 11-4. The Updated Constructor in **library/CMS/Content/Item/Abstract.php**

```
public function __construct ($page = null)
{
    $this->_pageModel = new Model_Page();
    if (null != $page) {
        $this->loadPageObject($page);
    }
}
```

Next you need to update the **loadPageObject()** method to evaluate the page argument. If it is a Zend_Db_Table_Row object, then it sets this as the row. Otherwise, it converts it into an integer and attempts to load the page table row, as shown in Listing 11-5.

Listing 11-5. The Updated **loadPageObject()** *Method*

```
public function loadPageObject ($page)
{
    if (is_object($page) && get_class ($page) == 'Zend_Db_Table_Row') {
        $row = $page;
        $this->id = $row->id;
    } else {
        $this->id = intval($page);
        $row = $this->_getInnerRow();
    }
     if ($row) {
        if ($row->namespace != $this->_namespace) {
            throw new Zend_Exception('Unable to cast page type:' . $row->namespace .
                ' to type:' . $this->_namespace);
        }
        $this->name = $row->name;
        $this->parent_id = $row->parent_id;
        $contentNode = new Model_ContentNode();
        $nodes = $row->findDependentRowset($contentNode);
        if ($nodes) {
            $properties = $this->_getProperties();
            foreach ($nodes as $node) {
                $key = $node['node'];
                if (in_array($key, $properties)) {
                    // try to call the setter method
                    $value = $this->_callSetterMethod($key, $nodes);
                    if ($value === self::NO_SETTER) {
                        $value = $node['content'];
                    }
                    $this->$key = $value;
                }
```

```
            }
        }
    } else {
        throw new Zend_Exception("Unable to load content item");
    }
}
```

Next you need to update the page controller so it passes the full row to the content item. This is a simple task; you just update the line in the open action, as shown in Listing 11-6.

Listing 11-6. Updating the Page Controller to Pass the Complete Row in application/controllers/PageController.php

```
if ($row) {
    $this->view->page = new CMS_Content_Item_Page($row);
```

Now when you refresh the page, you will see that you resolved two of the unnecessary queries, but it is still querying twice for the same page.

If you step through the code now, you will see that it is the menu controller that is doing this; it is loading a page object for each of the menu items. This adds a lot of flexibility in rendering the menus, so I would focus on caching the menu so it is not running these queries on every page view.

Caching

The CMS project that you have developed in this book builds a page directly from page data in the database. This gives you a great deal of control and flexibility, which is critical when you are building dynamic sites.

There is a downside, however. This is a resource-intensive process that is not always necessary. For example, the high-level site architecture (the main menu) is not likely to change very often. Using the dynamic approach, the server has to rebuild this menu every request, even though the underlying data is read much more than it is written. This makes the menu a prime candidate for caching.

Zend_Cache provides a generic interface for caching data that can work with a range of back-end technologies. It splits the caching responsibilities into two areas:

- Zend_Cache_Frontend is the interface that you program to.

- Zend_Cache_Backend manages the underlying cached data and how the system stores it.

Implementing Cache

To get started, you need to update your application to enable caching. You can do this in a few ways. The simplest method is to update the bootstrap file, adding a new _init*() function, as you did with the view and autoloader. In this section, I'll explain another approach to bootstrapping resources: creating Zend_Application resources themselves. By moving this function to its own application resource, you can reuse the resource in any Zend Framework project.

Configuring the Cache

A number of configuration options give you control over how the cache is handled by your application. First you need to set two general cache settings: where to store the front-end and back-end cache. Next you need to set the front-end options:

- `lifetime`: This is the length of time that the cache will persist. This is measured in seconds and defaults to 3600 (1 hour).

- `automatic_serialization`: This enables you to store data in the cache that is not in string form by serializing it. It is slower but makes reading and writing to the cache easier.

On the back end, you will need to set the following settings:

- `lifetime`: This is the same setting as the front-end option of the same name.

- `cache_dir`: This is the directory that the cache files will be stored in when you use a file-based back end.

■ **Note** In this example, you are going to use the most common settings, but I strongly recommend reviewing the current Zend Framework documentation; a number of methods for optimizing your site caching are beyond the scope of this book.

First you need to create a folder for the cache in the root of your project named `cache`. Then you will add these settings to the `application.ini` configuration file, as shown in Listing 11-7. `Zend_Application` will pass these settings to your application resource, enabling you to fine-tune the cache without altering your source code.

Listing 11-7. The Cache Settings in application/configs/application.ini

```
resources.cache.frontEnd = core
resources.cache.backEnd = file
resources.cache.frontEndOptions.lifetime = 1200
resources.cache.frontEndOptions.automatic_serialization = true
resources.cache.backEndOptions.lifetime = 3600
resources.cache.backEndOptions.cache_dir = APPLICATION_PATH "/../cache"
```

Creating the Cache Application Resource

The first step to create an application resource is to add a new folder to the library for your resources. Create a new folder in the `library/CMS` folder named `Application`. Then add a subfolder named `Resource` to this. Note that when I build library components, I try to follow the Zend Framework structure as much as possible. This makes it much easier for a developer who is experienced with the framework to find their way around your code.

Next you should add the path to the plug-in folder in the `application.ini` configuration file (see Listing 11-8) that tells the application where to look for additional plug-ins.

Listing 11-8. Adding the Resource Folder to the Application Configuration file in

application/configs/application.ini

```
pluginPaths.CMS_Application_Resource = APPLICATION_PATH
"/../library/CMS/Application/Resource"
```

Now you are ready to create the cache resource. Create a new file in the library/CMS/Application/Resource folder named `Cache.php`. Then create a class in this file named `CMS_Application_Resource_Cache`, which extends `Zend_Application_Resource_ResourceAbstract`.

When the application loads this resource, it will call the `init()` method. `Zend_Application` registers the return value of this method, so in this case you will create and configure the cache and return the cache object. This allows you to fetch the cache from `Zend_Application` using the `getResource('cache')` method. It is also a good idea to add the cache to the `Zend_Registry` so you can work with the cache without loading the application object.

In the case of this resource, most of the work is already done for you. `Zend_Cache` has a cache factory method. You pass this method your cache configuration options, and it builds the cache object for you, as shown in Listing 11-9.

Listing 11-9. The Cache Application Resource in library/CMS/Application/Resource/Cache.php

```php
<?php
class CMS_Application_Resource_Cache extends Zend_Application_Resource_ResourceAbstract
{
    public function init ()
    {
        $options = $this->getOptions();
        // Get a Zend_Cache_Core object
        $cache = Zend_Cache::factory(
            $options['frontEnd'],
            $options['backEnd'],
            $options['frontEndOptions'],
            $options['backEndOptions']);
        Zend_Registry::set('cache', $cache);
        return $cache;
    }
}
```

It is important to understand that the bootstrap object is not global. This means you need to fetch the bootstrap in order to access the registered resources. `Zend_Application_Bootstrap_Bootstrap` makes this easier by registering the bootstrap as a front controller parameter. This enables you to fetch the bootstrap at any point from your front controller using the `getInvokeArg('bootstrap')` method. I will demonstrate its usage in the next section.

Caching Menu Data

When you profiled the application, it became clear that the menus were running several queries on every page load. The site menus are not likely to change very often, which makes this a perfect use case for caching.

Caching data with Zend_Cache is a trivial task; you simply call the Zend_Cache save() method. The save() method takes three arguments:

- *The data to cache*: This data should be in string form, but since you turned the automatic_serialization option on, you can cache any form of data including arrays and objects. Zend_Cache handles *serializing* the data when you write to the cache and *unserializing* it when you fetch it back from the cache.

- *The cache key*: This is a unique identifier for the cached data. I try to use descriptive names, such as menu_1, where 1 is the primary key of the menu in the database.

- *Tags*: This is an array of tags, which enables you to categorize a cache entry. In this case, you will create a tag for each menu item so you can flush the menu from the cache when you update an item and leave other cache entries intact.

To get started, open the menu controller's render action. When you configured the cache with the cache application resource, it registered the Zend_Cache instance with the application. This is registered as a front controller parameter, so you can fetch it anywhere in your controllers. Fetch the bootstrap using the getInvokeArg('bootstrap') method, as shown in Listing 11-10. Then fetch the cache resource from the bootstrap, using the getResource('cache') method.

Now that you have the configured instance of Zend_Cache, you are ready to cache the menus. But first, you need to check whether the menu is already cached. If you find it in the cache, you simply pass the menu to the view. Otherwise, you need to load the menu and cache it.

Loading the menu into the cache is a very straightforward task; you simply build the menu and then save it to the cache using the save() method. Now you need to create an array of tags for each of the pages that the menu points to. You pass these tags to the save() method as the third argument. This enables you to find all the cache entries that are associated with a specific page so you can purge specific files from the cache when the page changes or is removed.

Listing 11-10. The Updated Render Menu Action in application/controllers/MenuController.php

```php
public function renderAction ()
{
    $menu = $this->_request->getParam('menu');
    // fetch the Zend_Cache object
    $bootstrap = $this->getInvokeArg('bootstrap');
    $cache = $bootstrap->getResource('cache');
    $cacheKey = 'menu_' . $menu;
    // attempt to load the menu from cache
    $container = $cache->load($cacheKey);
    if (! $container) {
        // if the menu is not cached then build it and cache it
        $mdlMenuItems = new Model_MenuItem();
        $menuItems = $mdlMenuItems->getItemsByMenu($menu);
        if (count($menuItems) > 0) {
            foreach ($menuItems as $item) {
```

```
                    // add a cache tag so you can update the menu when you update the items
                    $tags[] = 'menu_item_' . $item->id;
                    $label = $item->label;
                    if (! empty($item->link)) {
                        $uri = $item->link;
                    } else {
                        // add a cache tag to this menu so you can update the cached menu
                        // when you update the page
                        $tags[] = 'page_' . $item->page_id;
                        // update this to form more search engine friendly URLs
                        $page = new CMS_Content_Item_Page($item->page_id);
                        $uri = '/page/open/title/' . $page->name;
                    }
                    $itemArray[] = array('label' => $label , 'uri' => $uri);
                }
                $container = new Zend_Navigation($itemArray);
                // cache the container
                $cache->save($container, $cacheKey, $tags);
            }
        }
        if($container instanceof Zend_Navigation_Container) {
            $this->view->navigation()->setContainer($container);
        }
}
```

Now if you refresh the page that you profiled earlier, you will see the same results as on the earlier profile; it ran all the same queries. This is because it still runs the queries to build the cache. Now refresh the page again, and this time it should load the menu directly from the cache, without querying the database, as shown in Figure 11-2.

Database Profiling Report

Total queries executed: 5

Total elapsed time: 0.0045802593231201

#	Query	Time
(1) connect		0.0017199516296387
(2) DESCRIBE `pages`		0.0011720657348633
(3) SELECT `pages`.* FROM `pages` WHERE (name = 'Installing Zend Server') LIMIT 1		0.0002751350402832
(4) DESCRIBE `content_nodes`		0.0010459423065186
(5) SELECT `content_nodes`.* FROM `content_nodes` WHERE (`page_id` = 5)		0.00036716461181641

Figure 11-2. The page profile with the menu cached

Updating the Cached Menus

Instant gratification is a very important part of the user experience for your site managers. The cache is set to expire every 60 minutes, but when an administrator changes a menu, they expect to see the update immediately.

To do this, you need to update the application in a few areas, clearing the cached menu when you update the menu, one of its items, or one of the pages. To get started, open the Menu model's `updateMenu()` method.

■ **Note** This method of updating the cache will work only in single-machine configurations. For clusters or other multiple machine configurations, a more advanced updating method will be required. The first thing you need to do is fetch the cache. Since you are not doing this within the scope of the front controller, you will need to fetch it from the registry. Then you need to clean the menu from the cache so it will rebuild.

`Zend_Cache` has two methods for cleaning the cache:

- `remove()`: This removes a specific entry (by ID) from the cache.

- `clean()`: This method can remove multiple records, such as all the records with the `page_1` tag.

In this case you know the ID of the record, and you need to change only one record, so use the `remove()` method, as shown in Listing 11-11.

Listing 11-11. Removing the Cache Record When You Update a Menu in application/models/Menu.php

```
public function updateMenu($id, $name)
{
    $currentMenu = $this->find($id)->current();
    if($currentMenu) {
        // clear the cache entry for this menu
        $cache = Zend_Registry::get('cache');
        $id = 'menu_' . $id;
        $cache->remove($id);
        $currentMenu->name = $name;
        return $currentMenu->save();
    }else{
        return false;
    }
}
```

Next you need to update the menu item model, clearing the cached menu each time you modify its items, as shown in the `addItem()` method in Listing 11-12. Repeat this in each method that updates menu items.

Listing 11-12. Removing the Menu Cache Record When You Update a Menu Item in
application/models/MenuItem.php

```
public function addItem ($menuId, $label, $pageId = 0, $link = null)
{
    // clear the cache entry for the menu
    $cache = Zend_Registry::get('cache');
    $id = 'menu_' . $menuId;
    $cache->remove($id);

    $row = $this->createRow();
    $row->menu_id = $menuId;
    $row->label = $label;
    $row->page_id = $pageId;
    $row->link = $link;
    $row->position = $this->_getLastPosition($menuId) + 1;
    return $row->save();
}
```

You also need to update the cached menu when you update or remove one of the pages to which it points. When you cached the menu, you added tags for each of the pages that the menu references; now you need to update the page model, clearing any cache records that are tagged to a page when you update or delete it. Listing 11-13 demonstrates how to do this in the updatePage() method. Repeat this in the deletePage() method.

Listing 11-13. Clearing Cache Records That Are Tagged to a Page You Update in
application/models/Page.php

```
public function updatePage($id, $data)
{
    // find the page
    $row = $this->find($id)->current();
    if($row) {
        // clear any cache records which are tagged to this page
        $cache = Zend_Registry::get('cache');
        $tag = 'page_' . $id;
        $cache->clean(
            Zend_Cache::CLEANING_MODE_MATCHING_TAG,
            array($tag)
        );

        // update each of the columns that are stored in the pages table
        $row->name = $data['name'];
        $row->parent_id = $data['parent_id'];
        $row->save();
        // unset each of the fields that are set in the pages table
        unset($data['id']);
        unset($data['name']);
        unset($data['parent_id']);
        // set each of the other fields in the content nodes table
```

```
        if(count($data) > 0) {
            $mdlContentNode = new Model_ContentNode();
            foreach ($data as $key => $value) {
                $mdlContentNode->setNode($id, $key, $value);
            }
        }
    } else {
        throw new Zend_Exception('Could not open page to update!');
    }
}
```

Caching Content Items

Once you have cached the menus, there are five more queries when you open a page; these queries are being done by the content item when you load it. Since you turned automatic serialization on, you can cache any form of object, including the loaded content items.

To cache the loaded content item, open the page controller's open action. You will need to refactor this slightly to optimize it for the cache (Listing 11-14). The goal with caching the content is to minimize database traffic, but you do have one challenge; you still need to resolve a title to the page if the request passes a SEO-friendly URL. Time to refactor!

Now you need to test and see whether a title was passed. If it was, then resolve the title to the page. Once you have this page ID, you attempt to load the cached item as you did with the menu. If the item does not exist in the cache, then load it as you did with the menus and save it to the cache. You should tag this record with the page ID so it will reload if you make any changes to the page.

Listing 11-14. Updating the Open Page Action to Cache the Content Item in

application/controllers/PageController.php

```
public function openAction ()
{
    $title = $this->_request->getParam('title');
    $mdlPage = new Model_Page();
    $row = null;
    if (null !== $title) {
        $select = $mdlPage->select();
        $select->where('name = ?', $title);
        $row = $mdlPage->fetchRow($select);
        $id = $row->id;
    } else {
        $id = $this->_request->getParam('id');
    }

    // first confirm the page exists
    $bootstrap = $this->getInvokeArg('bootstrap');
    $cache = $bootstrap->getResource('cache');
    $cacheKey = 'content_page_' . $id;
    $page = $cache->load($cacheKey);
    if(!$page) {
        if($row instanceof Zend_Db_Table_Row) {
            $page = new CMS_Content_Item_Page($row);
```

```
    } else {
        $page = new CMS_Content_Item_Page($id);
    }
    // add a cache tag to this menu so you can update the cached menu
    // when you update the page
    $tags[] = 'page_' . $page->id;
    $cache->save($page, $cacheKey, $tags);
    }
    $this->view->page = $page;
}
```

Now if you refresh the page (twice), the profiler will disappear. That is because it displays only when there are queries to profile, and your application is now serving content without hitting the database.

Internationalization

It is becoming very common to have international teams of contributors working on a website together. Many people standardize their applications to use common languages, but this can limit the reach of your project.

Zend Framework supports many levels of internationalization. It gives you fine-grained control over the locale and character sets it uses, for example. In this section, I will focus multilingual applications.

Getting Started with Zend_Translate

Zend_Translate makes translating your ZF projects much easier than using the native PHP functions. It supports a range of source formats, has a very simple API, and tightly integrates with many ZF components such as Zend_View and Zend_Form.

Zend_Translate_Adapters

The first thing you need to do is determine which adapter you want to use. The adapters are in the same vein as those for Zend_Db_Table; they allow the common API to connect to a range of data sources.

In this example, you will use the CSV adapter. You can create the files with either a text editor or most spreadsheet programs.

Integrating Zend_Translate with Your Project

There are many ways to integrate Zend_Translate with your project, but I prefer to create application resources for any kind of generalized configuration like this. This enables you to reuse the resource in any ZF project you work on.

To get started, create a new folder in the application folder named lang. Then create two files in this folder: source-en.csv and source-es.csv.

■ **Note** It is not technically necessary to create a language file for your default language. If the translate helper does not locate a translation, it simply renders the text you pass it. I prefer to create one nonetheless because this file serves as a template for people who want to translate the application into their language of choice.

The next step is to update your `application.ini` configuration file, adding the adapter you want to use and the paths to your language files, as shown in Listing 11-15.

Listing 11-15. Adding the Translate Settings to `application/configs/application.ini`

```
resources.translate.adapter = csv
resources.translate.default.locale = "en_US"
resources.translate.default.file = APPLICATION_PATH "/lang/source-en.csv"
resources.translate.translation.es = APPLICATION_PATH "/lang/source-es.csv"
```

Now create a new file in `library/CMS/Application/Resource` named `Translate.php`. Create a new class named `CMS_Application_Resource_Translate` that extends `Zend_Application_Resource_ResourceAbstract`.

The translate application resource needs to create an instance of `Zend_Translate`, adding each of the translation files with their appropriate locales. Then it registers the `Zend_Translate` instance in `Zend_Registry` so the rest of the application can access it, as shown in Listing 11-16.

Listing 11-16. The Translation Application Resource in
`library/CMS/Application/Resource/Translate.php`

```php
<?php
class CMS_Application_Resource_Translate extends Zend_Application_Resource_ResourceAbstract
{
    public function init ()
    {
        $options = $this->getOptions();
        $adapter = $options['adapter'];
        $defaultTranslation = $options['default']['file'];
        $defaultLocale = $options['default']['locale'];
        $translate = new Zend_Translate($adapter, $defaultTranslation, $defaultLocale);
        foreach ($options['translation'] as $locale => $translation) {
            $translate->addTranslation($translation, $locale);
        }
        Zend_Registry::set('Zend_Translate', $translate);
        return $translate;
    }
}
```

Once this resource is configured, you are ready to start translating your interface. Translating the front end is a very straightforward task; `Zend_View` has a `translate()` helper, which automatically fetches the `Zend_Translate` instance from the registry. You simply pass the helper the string you want translated.

In this example, I will just translate the headline on the search box; you can follow this lead and translate the rest of the application.

Update application/layouts/scripts/layout.phtml, replacing the search box headline with the code in Listing 11-17.

Listing 11-17. Translating the Search Box Headline in application/layouts/scripts/layout.phtml

```
<div id='searchForm'>
    <h2><?php echo $this->translate('Search Site');?></h2>
    <?php
        $searchForm = new Form_SearchForm();
        $searchForm->setAction('/search');
        echo $searchForm->render();
    ?>
    <br />
</div>
```

Next you need to add Search Site to the language files, as shown in Listings 11-18 and 11-19.

Listing 11-18. The Translated Search Headline in application/lang/source-en.csv

```
"Search Site"; "Search Site"
```

Listing 11-19. The Translated Search Headline in application/lang/source-es.csv

```
"Search Site"; "Busca Sitio"
```

Now your CMS will render this text in the proper language, which Zend_Translate will determine based on the headers that the browser passes it.

Other Hidden Gems

Zend Framework has many other components that I do not have time to go over in this section. Some are very specific to certain classes of applications, while there are many more that can be used in a wide range of projects.

I learn something new every time I visit the Zend Framework site and recommend that you do the same.

Summary

You started this chapter by learning how to fine-tune your project to perform as quickly as possible. You stepped through profiling the application to identify bottlenecks. Then you optimized the core content item class to resolve one of the largest issues.

Once this was done, you went on to set up the CMS cache. After caching several of the items, you optimized the application to the point that it no longer queries the database at all for standard page views.

Next you learned about internationalization and set up your CMS to take advantage of `Zend_Translate`.

The subject matter covered in this chapter could have easily filled entire books, but I hope it gave you a taste of some of the lower-level features of the framework and provided a solid starting point for you to start exploring on your own.

CHAPTER 12

■ ■ ■

Installing and Managing a Site with Your CMS

In this chapter, I'll cover how to install and manage a site with your CMS.

Creating the Database

The first step to install your CMS on your production server is to create the database. Therefore, create a new database on your server using the MySQL command in Listing 12-1.

Listing 12-1. *Creating the CMS Database*

```
CREATE DATABASE cms_database
```

Once you create the database, you need to create a new user for the CMS database using the command in Listing 12-2. On your local server, you may have used the root MySQL user, but this is a critical security risk on a production database. Make sure you make a note of the user's credentials, because you will need to update the CMS configuration file when you install the application code base.

Listing 12-2. *Creating the CMS Database User*

```
CREATE USER 'cms_user'@'localhost' IDENTIFIED BY 'secret_password';
```

Grant the user permission to SELECT, INSERT, UPDATE, and DELETE on the cms_database database using the command in Listing 12-3.

Listing 12-3. *Granting the cms_user Access to the cms_database*

```
GRANT SELECT,INSERT,UPDATE,DELETE ON cms_database.* TO 'cms_user'@'localhost';
```

Now you are ready to install the database. Over the course of this book, you have built the database step-by-step, but when you install a new copy, it is more convenient to run a database dump script, which will install the whole, empty database, as in Listing 12-4. The only data that this dump script inserts is the default menus and the default site administrator account.

Listing 12-4. *The Database Dump for the CMS Database*

```
SET FOREIGN_KEY_CHECKS=0;
-- ---------------------------
-- Table structure for content_nodes
-- ---------------------------
DROP TABLE IF EXISTS `content_nodes`;
CREATE TABLE `content_nodes` (
  `id` int(11) NOT NULL auto_increment,
  `page_id` int(11) default NULL,
  `node` varchar(50) default NULL,
  `content` text,
  PRIMARY KEY  (`id`)
) ENGINE=InnoDB AUTO_INCREMENT=41 DEFAULT CHARSET=utf8;


-- ---------------------------
-- Table structure for menu_items
-- ---------------------------
DROP TABLE IF EXISTS `menu_items`;
CREATE TABLE `menu_items` (
  `id` int(11) NOT NULL auto_increment,
  `menu_id` int(11) default NULL,
  `label` varchar(250) default NULL,
  `page_id` int(11) default NULL,
  `link` varchar(250) default NULL,
  `position` int(11) default NULL,
  PRIMARY KEY  (`id`)
) ENGINE=InnoDB AUTO_INCREMENT=14 DEFAULT CHARSET=utf8;


-- ---------------------------
-- Table structure for menus
-- ---------------------------
DROP TABLE IF EXISTS `menus`;
CREATE TABLE `menus` (
  `id` int(11) NOT NULL auto_increment,
  `name` varchar(50) default NULL,
  `access_level` varchar(50) default NULL,
  PRIMARY KEY  (`id`)
) ENGINE=InnoDB AUTO_INCREMENT=6 DEFAULT CHARSET=utf8;


-- ---------------------------
-- Table structure for pages
-- ---------------------------
DROP TABLE IF EXISTS `pages`;
CREATE TABLE `pages` (
  `id` int(11) NOT NULL auto_increment,
  `parent_id` int(11) default NULL,
  `namespace` varchar(50) default NULL,
  `name` varchar(100) default NULL,
  `date_created` int(11) default NULL,
  PRIMARY KEY  (`id`)
```

```
) ENGINE=InnoDB AUTO_INCREMENT=11 DEFAULT CHARSET=utf8;

-- ----------------------------
-- Table structure for users
-- ----------------------------
DROP TABLE IF EXISTS `users`;
CREATE TABLE `users` (
  `id` int(11) NOT NULL auto_increment,
  `username` varchar(50) default NULL,
  `password` varchar(250) default NULL,
  `first_name` varchar(50) default NULL,
  `last_name` varchar(50) default NULL,
  `role` varchar(25) default NULL,
  PRIMARY KEY  (`id`)
) ENGINE=InnoDB AUTO_INCREMENT=2 DEFAULT CHARSET=utf8;

-- ----------------------------
-- Records
-- ----------------------------
INSERT INTO `menu_items` VALUES ('1', '1', 'Home', '0', '/', '1');
INSERT INTO `menu_items` VALUES ('2', '2', 'Manage Content', '0', '/page/list', '1');
INSERT INTO `menu_items` VALUES ('3', '2', 'Manage Menus', '0', '/menu', '2');
INSERT INTO `menu_items` VALUES ('4', '2', 'Manage Users', '0', '/user/list', '3');
INSERT INTO `menu_items` VALUES ('5', '2', 'Rebuild Search Index', '0', ↵
 '/search/build', '4');
INSERT INTO `menus` VALUES ('1', 'main_menu', null);
INSERT INTO `menus` VALUES ('2', 'admin_menu', null);
INSERT INTO `users` VALUES ('1', 'admin', '5f4dcc3b5aa765d61d8327deb882cf99', 'test',
'user', 'Administrator');
```

Installing the Application

Once your database is installed and configured, you are ready to install the application. Your directory structure may depend on your server configuration, but in most hosting situations you will have a public document root for your server named www or public_html. Upload all the files that are in your application's public directory into this directory.

Next you need to upload the application and library files. The application and library directories should not be directly accessible by the public. Upload these directories to the root of your hosting account, which should be next to the document root, as in Listing 12-5.

Listing 12-5. *Standard Directory Structure for Your CMS*

```
/ account root
  /public_html
  /application
  /library
```

Alternate Installations

You can alternatively put your library and application directories in any location that is accessible by your web server. Simply update your application, and include the paths in your index.php file.

Sharing One Common Library

If you are hosting this CMS on a dedicated server, you may want to be able to share a common Zend Framework library. You can move the Zend directory from your application's library to the directory specified in your server's PHP include path.

■ **Note** As the framework evolves, which is quite a rapid process, you may not want to be tied to using one specific version of the framework. What I do is create subdirectories in the include directory like ZF_1_8. I then add this to my include path in the index.php file.

Configuring Your CMS

The only configuration that you will likely need to do to your CMS is to update the application.ini file by updating the database connection information, as in Listing 12-6. I also turn the profiler off.

Listing 12-6. Setting Your Production Database Connection in application/configs/application.ini

```
resources.db.adapter = "pdo_mysql"
resources.db.params.host = "localhost"
resources.db.params.username = "cms_user"
resources.db.params.password = "secret_password"
resources.db.params.dbname = "cms_database"
resources.db.params.profiler = false
resources.db.isDefaultTableAdapter = true
```

Then set your application environment to production in .htaccess, as in Listing 12-7.

Listing 12-7. Setting the Application Environment in public_html/.htaccess

```
SetEnv APPLICATION_ENV production
```

Managing Users

Once your CMS is installed and configured, the first thing you should do is log in and update the admin user account. The default database installation script (Listing 12-4) creates a user with the following credentials:

- *Username*: admin

- *Password*: password

To get to the login page, click the link under My Account in the sidebar. Then go to /user/list. You should see the user table, as in Figure 12-1.

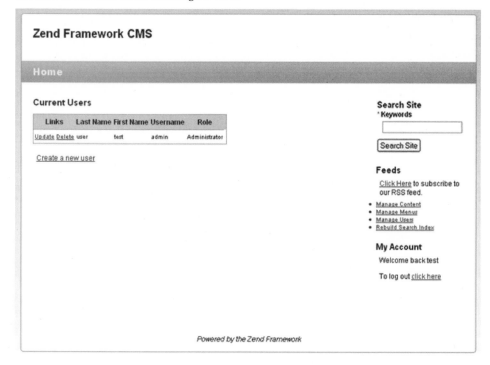

Figure 12-1. *The manage users page*

Creating a User

You can either create a new user and delete the default user or just update the default user account. I will create a new user. Click the "Create a new user" link beneath the user table. This will open the create user form (see Figure 12-2). Create the user, and click Submit.

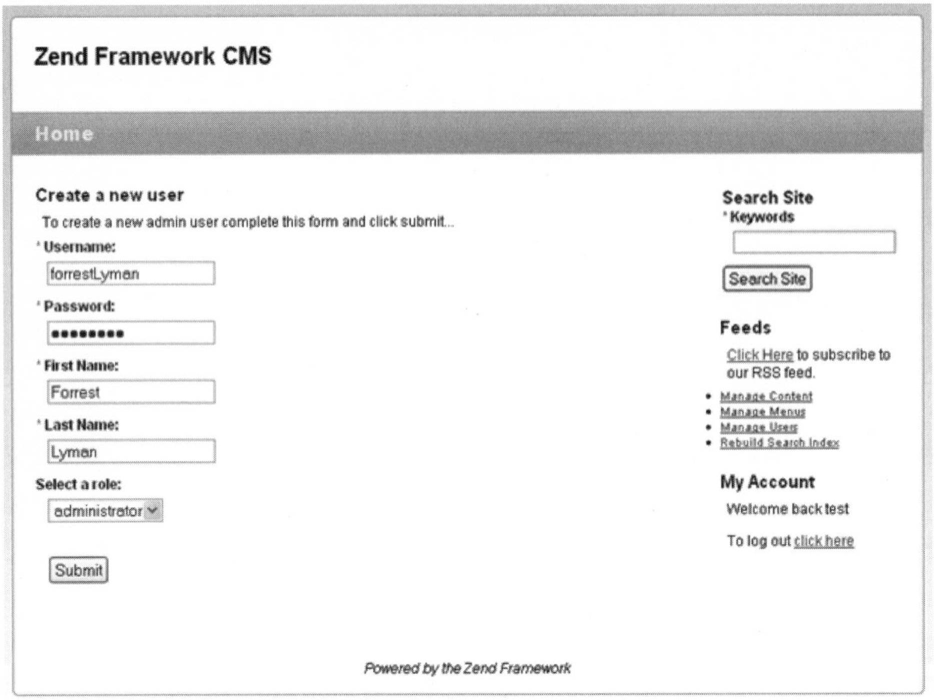

Figure 12-2. Creating a user account

Updating a User

To update a user account, click the Update link next to their name in the user table. The update user form is virtually identical to the create user form, except there is no field to update the user's password. To update the user's password, click the Update Password link below the Submit button.

Deleting a User

Once you have created your user account, you should delete the default account. Click the Delete link next to the default user's name in the user table.

Managing Content

Now that you have secured your CMS installation, you are ready to start working with content. Click the Manage Content link on the sidebar to get started.

Creating a Page

When you click the Manage Content link, you will see a message that you do not have any pages yet. Click the "Create a new page" link beneath this. This will open the page form (see Figure 12-3). Fill out the page form, and click Submit to create it. Once your page is created, you will be directed back to the page/list page. The page will now display a table with your new page in it.

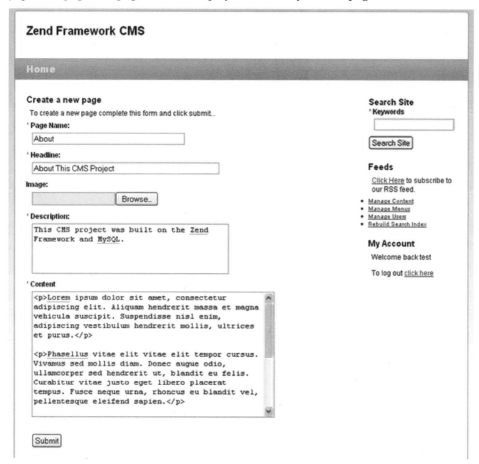

Figure 12-3. The create page form

Updating a Page

When you need to update a page, you go to /page/list. Click the Update link next to the page that you want to update. The update form will open (which is identical to the create page form). Make any changes you need, and click Submit to save them.

Deleting a Page

To delete a page, click the Delete link next to the page name in the page list.

Navigating Between Pages

Now you need to add your new page to the site navigation. Click the Manage Menus link in the sidebar. You will see a table with the current menus, as in Figure 12-4.

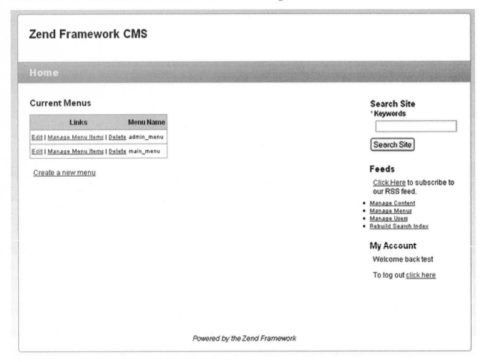

Figure 12-4. The manage menus page

Adding a Menu Item

To add your page to the main menu, click the Manage Menu Items link in the main_menu row. This will open the menu items list for the main_menu. Click "Add a new item." This will open the add item form (see Figure 12-5).
There are two types of menu items: static links and direct links to existing pages. In this example, you are adding a link to the page that you just created, so you select the page from the drop-down list. Once you have done this, click Submit to create the menu item.

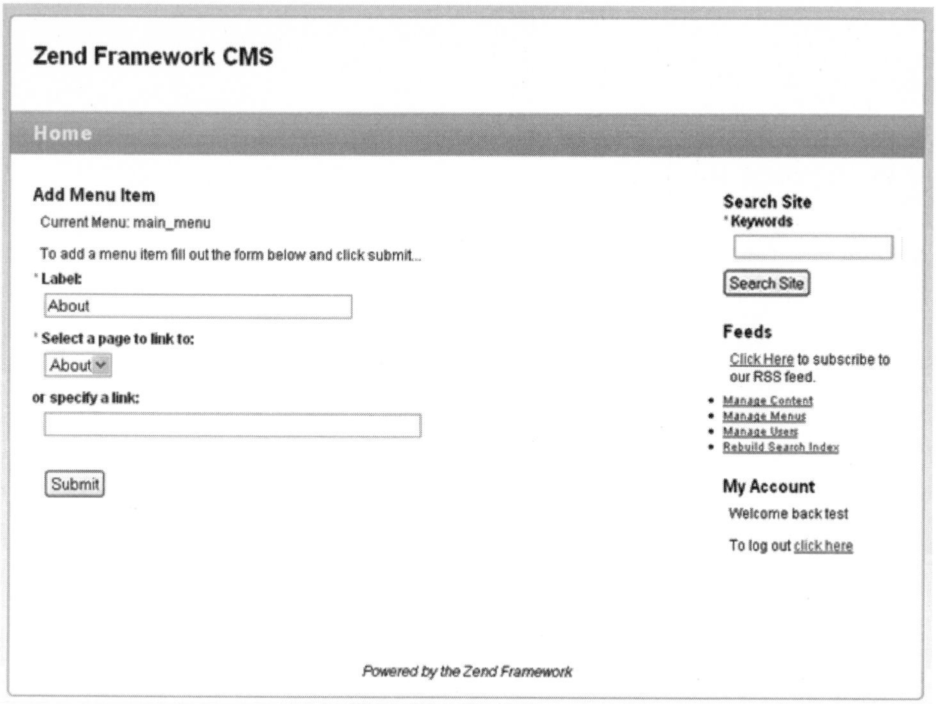

Figure 12-5. *Adding a page to a menu*

Sorting Menu Items

In this case, your new menu item will be inserted after the Home link, which is probably what you want. When you do need to reorder a menu, you can do so in the Manage Menu Items table. You will notice that there are Move Up and Move Down links next to the menu items (see Figure 12-6). Clicking these will sort your menu items.

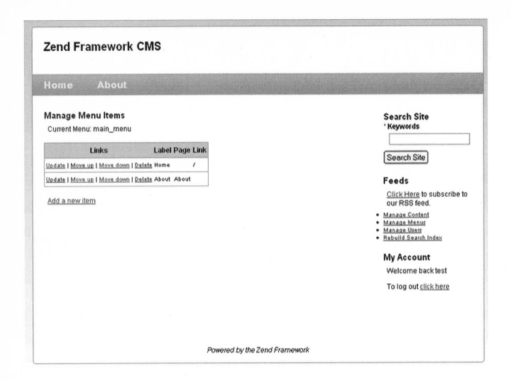

Figure 12-6. *The Manage Menu Items list*

Updating Menu Items

To update a menu item, go to the manage menu items page. Click the Update link next to the item that you want to update. The update form will open, which is identical to the create menu item form.

Deleting Menu Items

To remove a menu item, go to the manage menu items page. Click the Delete link next to the item that you want to remove.

The Next Steps

The CMS project I guided you through building in this book was very simplistic by design. I wanted to focus on the underlying technologies rather than show you how to build the next best CMS solution. I also think that the simpler software is, the easier it is to customize.

Over the course of this project, you learned how to work with many Zend Framework components. Between this foundation of experience and the online Zend Framework resources, you should be well on your way to becoming a proficient CMS developer.

Index

You Need the Companion eBook

Your purchase of this book entitles you to buy the companion PDF-version eBook for only $10. Take the weightless companion with you anywhere.

We believe this Apress title will prove so indispensable that you'll want to carry it with you everywhere, which is why we are offering the companion eBook (in PDF format) for $10 to customers who purchase this book now. Convenient and fully searchable, the PDF version of any content-rich, page-heavy Apress book makes a valuable addition to your programming library. You can easily find and copy code—or perform examples by quickly toggling between instructions and the application. Even simultaneously tackling a donut, diet soda, and complex code becomes simplified with hands-free eBooks!

Once you purchase your book, getting the $10 companion eBook is simple:

❶ Visit **www.apress.com/promo/tendollars/**.

❷ Complete a basic registration form to receive a randomly generated question about this title.

❸ Answer the question correctly in 60 seconds, and you will receive a promotional code to redeem for the $10.00 eBook.

eBookshop

233 Spring Street, New York, NY 10013

Offer valid through 4/10.